W9-AYW-378

Grief Ministry Facilitator's Guide

JoAnn Sturzl &
Donna Reilly Williams

Resource Publications, Inc.
San Jose, California

Editorial director: Kenneth Guentert
Managing editor: Elizabeth J. Asborno
Cover design and production: Huey Lee

© 1992 Resource Publications, Inc. All rights reserved.
Permission is granted to photocopy only those handout pages
designated with this symbol: 🤲 .

For permission to duplicate or reprint any other part of this book,
write to:

Reprint Department
Resource Publications, Inc.
160 E. Virginia Street #290
San Jose, CA 95112-5876

Library of Congress Cataloging in Publication Data
Sturzl, JoAnn, 1933-
    Grief ministry facilitator's guide / JoAnn Sturzl & Donna Reilly
Williams.
        p.   cm.
    ISBN 0-89390-227-6
    1. Church work with the bereaved.   I. Williams, Donna
Reilly, 1945- .   II. Title
    BV4330.S88   1992   91-44883
259'.6—dc20   CIP

5 4 3 2 1 | 96 95 94 93 92

Excerpts from THE NEW JERUSALEM BIBLE, copyright © 1985 by
Darton, Longman & Todd, Ltd. and Doubleday, a division of
Bantam, Doubleday, Dell Publishing Group, Inc. Reprinted by
permission.

Excerpt from WHEN BAD THINGS HAPPEN TO GOOD PEOPLE by
Harold S. Kushner Copyright © 1981 by Harold S. Kushner.
Reprinted by permission of Schocken Books, published by
Pantheon Books, a division of Random House, Inc.

Contents

Introduction

How to Use This Book 1

Session 1

Introduction: Ministry Gifts and Call 7

Session 2

Death in Our Society: Grief as Life Transition 10

Session 3

The Grief Journey 13

Session 4

Experiencing Pain: Sympathy/Empathy 16

Session 5

Person-to-Person Skills 19

Session 6

Prayer and Spiritual Resources 21

Session 7

Depression and Suicide:
Trusting Your Pastoral Intuitions 24

Session 8

Children and Loss: Death of a Baby 27

Session 9

Divorce and Other Life Transitions 30

Session 10

Rites and Services: Commissioning Service 33

Appendix A: Handouts

Handout 1

The Call to Grief Ministry 41

Handout 2

Death Inventory 45

Handout 3

Natural Life Transitions 47

Handout 4

The Life Continuum 51

Handout 5

Thoughts or Feelings? 53

Handout 6

The Grief Process 57

Handout 7

The Use of Energy While Grieving 59

Handout 8

The Gift of Love (Jewish Version) 61

Handout 8

The Gift of Love (Christian Version) 65

Handout 9

It Helps to Have Friends Who Will Listen 69

Handout 10

Companions for the Journey 71

Handout 11

Trusting Your Pastoral Intuitions 73

Handout 12

What Good, Then, Is Religion? 75

Appendix B: Exercises

Exercise 1
Group Listening Exercise (A) 79

Exercise 2
Group Listening Exercise (B) 81

Exercise 3
Role Playing Exercise 83

Exercise 4
Lemon Exercise 85

Exercise 5
Scenarios for Discussion 87

Exercise 6
Scenarios for Role Playing 89

Appendix C: Meditations

Meditation 1
Pictures of Pain 93

Meditation 2
God Speaks 99

Meditation 3
Words to "Someone Who'll Stay" 101

Appendix D: Guest Speaker's Preparation Sheet **103**

Appendix E:
Evaluation of Grief Ministry Training Program **105**

Appendix F: Prayer Request Card **107**

Resources **109**

How to Use This Facilitator's Guide

When we (JoAnn and Donna) met several years ago, we both felt a special excitement and that strange, exhilarating sense one occasionally experiences that this meeting was very much "of God." Neither of us knew why, and for a while, it was enough to enjoy each other as "kindred spirits," and to develop our plans for training parish pastoral ministers. It was fun to work together and enriching to be gifted with those who participated in our programs.

Then one day, we looked at each other and said, "We should put this into a book so others can be gifted as we have." Neither of us can remember who first spoke the idea, but it arose from both of our hearts. This manual, and the textbook on which it is based, are the fruit of that moment, and we believe that God has led, blessed, and inspired us in their writing. As we have moved together through the process, we have had chances to minister to each other in moments of intense pain. This program is a labor of love, mingled with hope, tears, and hugs. We hope that it will make your teaching and facilitating tasks easier, as we have ironed out some of the problems. We also hope that, if you discover something that should be included, you will let us know. You are important to us, as you use this program. Because of that, we have included the prayer request card in Appendix F. For some of you, leading a program to train grief ministers will be a completely new experience. We want you to know that you are not alone, and we would love to join you in prayer as you carry out your first program.

In this manual, you will find plans for ten sessions. Each session contains Scripture/prayer components, affective (feeling) components, and didactic (intellectual) components. We have used current insights about both adult spirituality and adult learning styles, and we believe the program reflects the best contemporary insights about psycho/social/theological aspects of grieving and about pastoral ministry. The growth experienced through a program such as this is appropriate both for professionals who care for those who mourn and for volunteers in faith communities and hospitals.

Hints for Facilitation

Participants: Think of these adult learners as "participants," not as "students." You are there to facilitate their growth, not to teach. This difference in attitude reflects your respect for the people who come to the program as well as your conviction that without their contributions, the whole group will lose. Also, the responsibility for growth lies with each person, and while you are there for support, you cannot force them to be open and personally vulnerable. This aspect of the program is one of the most vital components.

At the end of the program, it is not necessary to "examine" participants to determine how they have grown. This will be obvious from their positive attitude toward ministries that were previously frightening and from their increased confidence in approaching people—even strangers—in times of crisis. They can now trust that their intuitions and skills are sufficient to minister constructively, no matter what situation develops.

We suggest that between ten and twenty participants is ideal for this program. This number allows for plenty of group action, but is still small enough for intimate sharing. A difficulty with having more than twenty participants is that when you break into small groups for sharing, there are too many groups for one facilitator to watch. Small group discussions, especially on topics that encourage avoidance, will not be very fruitful unless they are facilitated with some skill. So, especially if you are offering this program for the first time, we do discourage you from taking too many participants.

Remember that different people have differing learning styles, from those who take in every spoken word, to those who are mainly visual learners or who need an experiential medium. That is why the sessions are planned with so much variety; this will facilitate the growth of participants.

Session Timing: We prefer that the program be offered in ten two-hour sessions, so that is how the manual is designed. We have presented it over timespans varying from sixteen to twenty hours, and in conformations varying from evening sessions to weekends. Remember that for every break of more than forty-eight hours, some time must be taken to allow for reviewing and processing of what has happened in the hearts of individual participants.

We prefer ten sessions because the lapse of time between important concepts and experiences allows participants to internalize what has happened before moving on to something new. The break also allows time for people to read the appropriate chapters of *Grief Ministry*. However, time is not always available, so if you need to present the program during weekends, allow for reflective time between presentations and activities. This means that you will actually need to have participants together for more than the twenty hours prescribed. Eight or ten consecutive hours of this material would be exhausting and overload participants, so you need to take several long breaks. You may need to choose between the optional topics in the last few session plans, presenting the rest in refresher programs at another time. We strongly believe that it is more important to *properly deal with less material than to inflict overloads upon volunteers, who may then turn away from this sort of ministry.*

It is a welcome addition to the program if you invite guest speakers. Not only do guests add variety and new thoughts, but they can become resource persons for your participants' future ministries. Be sure to check with speakers in advance about the payment of a stipend.

Group Dynamics: As suggested earlier, small group discussions, if properly facilitated, can be fruitful. If you do choose this dynamic, we find four to be the ideal number. This is a large enough group not to frighten those who are reticent about intimacy, but small enough so everyone can speak comfortably.

Try to have a person in each group who can monitor if there is a "monopolizer" and who can encourage shy participants. If this is not possible, then you should move from group to group, becoming aware of the dynamics of each and dealing with problems before another small group session.

In large or small groups, all participants should have a chance to share their thoughts and feelings. Since some people are not secure with group sharing, you may need to encourage them with questions like, "Joe, I've seen you nodding as others shared. Would you like to tell us about your thoughts and feelings as we share on this topic?" or "Margaret, I see tears in your eyes. Would it help to share with us where those tears are coming from?"

The opposite problem is that every group has at least one monopolizer who will go over and over the same topic or hold the group's attention on a "red herring" that has very little to do with the topic of discussion. It is your responsibility to limit such sharing with statements like, "Thank you, Peter. That was very interesting. I'm sure some people would like to hear more about your experience at break time. Right now, we have to move on. John, did you have something to share?"

Never rush past the moment when a participant's pain brings on tears or sobs. Think of these times as especially graced and use them as opportunities for the group to minister to each other. The modeling you do at these moments will stay in the minds of all participants. If there is a serious emotional breakdown, call for a coffee break and spend some intimate time with the wounded person, determining if s/he should continue with the session, be referred for professional help, etc.

Thoughts and Feelings: One area of growth for many participants in this program is in learning to tell the difference between thoughts and feelings. This growth will be gradual, but the first session begins to ask questions about feelings and to allow people to reflect on what is "going on inside of them." Many people are not used to listening to their own internal messages, to what their bodies and psyches are telling them. Ministers can get into trouble if they respond to hurting people out of their own subconscious needs or feelings, which may be completely different from the feelings and thoughts of the person to whom they are called to minister. That is why so much of the emphasis of this program is on facilitating participants in becoming more aware of their own needs and motivations.

During the first session, do not correct participants if they confuse feelings with thoughts. But in the next session, explain the difference and ask participants to try to decide whether they are relating mainly out of thoughts or feelings.

A thought happens with the brain; it often takes the form of a judgment. However, people often voice thoughts as feelings: "I feel that this person should..."; "I feel that John is a friendly man." One clue to tell if we are really voicing a thought is the word "that.". Feelings do not usually have "that" in them: "I feel angry"; "I feel cold"; "I feel like a small girl again."

One reason people often voice thoughts as feelings is that a thought evokes strong feelings, and the person then uses the thought to express the feeling. But people in ministry need to learn to find the feeling that happens in response to the thought, and to name that feeling.

It is important that participants learn that we do not judge any feelings as "bad." There is no morality to feelings. Feelings just *are*. Society has labeled certain feelings, especially anger and sadness, as "bad." Good ministers realize that this label is inhibiting to hurting persons and can only cause problems in journeying through the grief process.

Encourage participants to be open to their own feelings about grief, loss, and dying, and to trust that these feelings—whatever they are—are valid and natural. During the program, many people will become aware of unhealed wounds from death/loss experiences. For the facilitator, this can be a reminder of the powerful surge toward healing in the human person and of the fact that it is never too late for this healing to happen.

Scripture/Prayer Components: In the outline for each session, there is a choice from either the First or Second Testament. While this choice offers freedom to Jewish facilitators, we encourage Christians to also use some of the readings from the First Testament. Much of Christianity's historical pain and healing as a faith group comes from Jewish roots, and it is important that this part of the story not be neglected.

We suggest that, after the first meeting, you encourage participants to take turns presenting this part of the sessions. You may want to give them the choice about which Scripture passage to use, and do give them a copy of that section of the session guide. Of course, you may choose to use completely different passages from those we cite; Scripture is so rich that we could never list all appropriate passages for a topic.

Environment: The environment in which the program is presented can detract from or add to the experience. We like to use candles, soft lights, prominent display of Scripture, quiet music as a background to reflection, and the natural enjoyment of fresh air in the room. If participants sense that you have gone to some trouble to prepare the meeting space, they will be more willing to personally risk and grow through the program.

Refreshments: Do have these, possibly at the end of the sessions, so people can unwind before driving home. You can choose when to take breaks, if you prefer to have refreshments in the middle of the sessions. If you do not use ten sessions and have participants together for long periods, plan a break every ninety minutes. You might want to have a participant bring snack foods. Keep in mind that not everyone drinks caffeine beverages; it is a good idea to also have juice and ice water available. If you will have long sessions, plan low-cal snacks and avoid high-sugar foods and drinks, which do not agree with many people's metabolism.

Handouts: Everything in appendices A, B, and C is for your use. Feel free to copy what you need. We ask you not to change wording or use only parts of handouts, as contexts can easily be changed, which opens possibilities for misunderstanding.

Audiovisual Aids: Details for ordering the recommended films and cassettes are included in the Resources section. We suggest that you make inquiries of local film libraries, who may have some of the resources. They might also suggest alternatives, but we urge you to be very selective about substitutions, which may not have the components appropriate for this program. Nancy Reeves' videos are available on a rental basis and contain material not available elsewhere, and the filmstrip *If I Should Die Before I Wake* is not expensive. *Always preview films before the class session* to be sure you are familiar with the contents.

We recommend the use of Deanna Edwards' music cassettes. There is a therapeutic content in these songs that is helpful in grief ministry as well as other areas of pastoral ministry.

Use a cassette player with clear sound so participants do not need to strain to hear words and so the music can touch people's hearts deeply. If you do not have a good player available, a participant will likely be willing to bring one.

Homework: At the end of each session, assign as homework reading the same chapters you pre-read in preparation. Assign the homework after you have taught the sessions, not before, so participants will achieve maximum enjoyment and benefit from each session.

Ongoing Support: The facilitator should always be available by phone in case participants need to talk about feelings or thoughts that have risen to the surface of their consciousness. Repeat this invitation as you say goodbye each week.

Those of us who have served as facilitators of this program have developed a new humility in the face of the compassion, insight, and courage of participants. Because of this, we have a greater commitment to minister holistically and to become more vulnerable to those we touch each day.

We hope our work will be useful to you. More than that, we hope you experience the joy and promise we have found in enabling others to find their own sources of strength and to minister from their hearts.

> The Spirit of Lord Yahweh is on me,
> He has sent me to bring the news to the afflicted,
> to soothe the broken hearted,
> to comfort all who mourn.
> (Isaiah 61:1-2)

Introduction:
Ministry Gifts and Call

Purpose   To create an atmosphere for learning, trust, and confidentiality.

To explore the call to ministry, based on gifts of person.

Materials

- ☐ Bible and candle
- ☐ Copies of Handout 1, "The Call to Grief Ministry" and Handout 2, "Death Inventory"
- ☐ Audio cassette player

- ☐ Box of tissues
- ☐ Audio cassette (your choice of music for the closing prayer)
- ☐ *Grief Ministry* textbook for each participant

- ☐ Filmstrip projector
- ☐ Filmstrip *Continuing the Ministry of Jesus* or similar resource

Preparation

- Read and understand Chapter 1 of *Grief Ministry* and Handout 1.
- Prepare a talk on personal gifts and the call to ministry.
- Set up filmstrip in projector and make sure audio cassette music for the closing prayer is ready to play.
- Invite two people who have been in person-to-person ministries to speak briefly to the group, and help them prepare their presentations.

Introduction and Overview

» Welcome participants and introduce yourself by sharing a bit of your own history and why you want to present this program.

» Invite each participant to introduce him/herself by telling why they are here or by sharing hopes for the program, and how they are feeling (excited, nervous, etc.).

» Thank each person and give a brief, affirming response (something like, "Thanks for sharing that; I'm sure many of us can identify with your feelings").

» Talk about the importance of confidentiality within the group.

» Give a brief overview of the program and what topics will be covered, what skills stressed. Emphasize that this is not a grief support group, but support will be provided to them if they uncover painful areas of grieving within themselves.

» Hand out the textbook and give them five minutes to look through it.

Prayer   *Isaiah 42:6-7 or Matthew 9:35-37*

These readings tell about God's desire to comfort, heal, and be with persons in need.

» After the reading, ask participants if anything especially touched them or spoke to their hearts.

» Invite each participant to share an experience of being touched and healed by God.

» Pray together a prayer appropriate to your faith group.

Instruction   » Speak on the call to minister to hurting members of the community. (Use as resources pages 1 and 2 of the text and Handout 1.)

» Show filmstrip *Continuing The Ministry Of Jesus* or a similar resource.

» Speak on identifying and using personal gifts, based on Chapter 1, pages 7-14 of *Grief Ministry*.

» Ask your invited guests to tell their stories, including what they do, how they became involved, and how it has affected their lives.

Experiential   » Have participants do two or three exercises from pages 12 and 13 of the text, then share their responses in small groups. Remind them of the need for confidentiality.

Homework   » Ask participants to read the Introduction and Chapter 1 of *Grief Ministry*.

» Give them Handout 1 and ask them to read it.

» Give them Handout 2; ask them to gradually and reflectively fill it out over the week. Stress that they are doing this for themselves and will not be asked to share their reflections unless they choose to do so.

» Invite a volunteer to do the opening prayer next session, and hand that person a copy of the appropriate section of the session plan.

Closing Prayer

» Play an inspirational hymn that speaks of the call to minister to others. (For Christian groups, we recommend "St. Theresa's Prayer" from John Michael Talbot's *Quiet Reflections*.)

» Briefly ask God's blessing on group members, especially as they reflect on their homework.

Death in Our Society: Grief as Life Transition

Purpose
To allow participants time to review their experiences with the "Death Inventory."

To examine some common attitudes about loss and grief.

To begin to understand the difference between thoughts and feelings.

Materials

- ☐ Bible and candle
- ☐ Copies of Handout 3, "Natural Life Transitions"; Handout 4, "The Life Continuum"; and Handout 5, "Thoughts/Feelings"

- ☐ Box of tissues
- ☐ Blackboard and chalk or similar setup for writing

- ☐ Audio cassette player
- ☐ Audio cassette *Peacebird* (Deanna Edwards)

Preparation

- Read and understand chapters 2 and 3 and pages 71-75 in *Grief Ministry*.
- Prepare a brief talk, using experiences from your own life, to illustrate the difference between thoughts and feelings.
- Set "Peacebird" at *Teach Me To Die*.

Prayer
Ecclesiastes 3:1-8 or John 11:1-7,17-37

Both these readings stress the healthiness of expressing emotions. Ecclesiastes says that anger, tears, laughter, dancing, and hatred are all appropriate emotions or expressions of emotion, in their own time.

In John's Gospel, Jesus models that even though he is God and knows that Lazarus will rise in this life, he is touched by the pain of his friends and, with them, he hurts and weeps. The women show that people of faith do grieve and feel anger. Jesus, who understands their normal expressions of grief, does not judge them harshly.

» Pray together, that participants may have "hearts of flesh" (Ezekiel 36:26) so that "we will all be sensitive to each other and to the pain in people's hearts."

Experiential » Invite participants to briefly share what has happened in their lives this week.

Did the readings touch them in any special way?

Did they have any striking thoughts or feelings as they filled out the "Death Inventory?" (Using the phrase "thoughts *or* feelings" will begin to call attention to the difference between them.)

» You might want to break into small groups to discuss a question like, "What was my experience with the homework?" Stress that the depth of their sharing is optional and their privacy will be respected, but invite each person to share at least one thing about the homework.

Instruction » Moving from the experiential discussion, explain that the "Death Inventory" was designed to help them examine some of their own attitudes about aging, loss, and grief. Explain that our society does not encourage examination of these attitudes. Ask participants to suggest some reasons why people shy away from these topics. As they are sharing, write brief notes on the blackboard. (In your own mind, be thinking about which reasons are thoughts or attitudes and which are feelings. You will use this later.)

Mention the differences in attitudes about death in different contemporary cultures. Ask participants if they have ever experienced grief expressed by someone from a culture different from their own. If you have a multi-cultural faith community, you might want to explore what that means for ministry. You might also reflect on how different age groups within your community deal differently with loss.

» Present the concept that we are experiencing loss throughout life. Distribute Handout 3, "Natural Life Transitions." Ask participants to read it and place a mark beside any transition that has significance in their own lives. (Tell them this is private; they will not need to share their observations.) After they have done this, explain that this program is designed to deal with "whole life grief"—that is, one's responses to all the transitions in life. The person who deals with minor transitions honestly and openly is better prepared to move through major loss and grief healthfully. The person who has never expressed the pain of past losses and transitions will have a harder task dealing with present grief.

Give them Handout 4, "The Life Continuum" and explain it, saying that this is why it is so important to allow ourselves and others to experience *whatever* is experienced in grief times.

» Now move to "how we experience grief." We do this two ways: by thoughts and by feelings. (Actions can express either thoughts or feelings.) Go back to what you wrote on the blackboard and help the group decide which observations were thoughts, which feelings. This may be difficult at first. Tell them they will get better at knowing the difference, and explain why it is one of the most vital skills for this ministry. Keep this part of the session fairly brief, as they will have a chance to practice with their homework.

Experiential   » Briefly remind participants:

> "There are two reasons why we come to these sessions. One is to help other people who are grieving. But in order to do that, we must honestly deal with our own mortality and feelings about death. People usually find that as we come to feel more comfortable with death, we see new beauty and depth in life. I am going to play a song about that growth when a person who is dying, as we all are, asks to learn what that means in order to better understand the meaning of life. Listen now to the song, and let it speak to you."

» Play "Teach Me To Die" (*Peacebird*). Allow a brief time after the song in case people need to share how it touched them.

Homework   » Give them Handout 5, "Thoughts/Feelings" and ask them to complete it during the week.

» Assign chapters 2 and 3 in *Grief Ministry* as reading homework.

» Invite a volunteer to do the opening prayer next session, and hand that person a copy of the appropriate section of the session plan.

Closing Prayer   » Invite participants to join hands and to pray for each other and for those they know are grieving.

The Grief Journey

Purpose   To understand the reason people grieve and the duration and dynamics of the grief process.

Materials

- ☐ Bible and candle
- ☐ Filmstrip projector
- ☐ Filmstrip *If I Should Die Before I Wake*

- ☐ Box of tissues
- ☐ Audio cassette player
- ☐ Audio cassette of soft instrumental music

- ☐ Blackboard and chalk

- ☐ Copies of Handout 6, "The Grief Process" and Handout 7, "Grief Energy Cycle"

Preparation

- Read to understand chapters 4 and 5 in *Grief Ministry*. (If you have a copy from the first printing, there is an error on the chart on page 59. The second and third circles should be interchanged. Use the copy in this manual.)
- Prepare a brief talk outlining pages 33-35.
- Be sure you understand the Grief Energy Cycle, so you can briefly explain it without having to refer to the text.

Prayer   *Isaiah 40:28-29 or John 4:4-26*

The first reading illustrates the fidelity of God, who will abide steadfastly with the mourner for as long as grief lasts. We as ministers are called to mirror this fidelity.

The second reading shows how, in approaching the Samaritan woman, Jesus broke down barriers of gender and race, and without judging, simply told her what he saw in her. He made her the offer of salvation before he told her he knew her personal story, so she felt accepted and ran to tell her friends the good news. We as ministers are challenged to also accept every person and, through our presence, to invite them into the love of God.

Instruction

» Give your brief talk to illustrate why people grieve. Then write on the blackboard,

Grief is the emotional, physical, and spiritual reaction to the loss (or perceived loss) of someone (or something) in whom (or which) one has been deeply emotionally invested.

» Allow about ninety seconds for participants to read and digest this information.

» Now ask them to think about a major life transition they have personally experienced. (You may want to refer them to Handout 3.) Invite them to try to remember emotional feelings, physical and mental symptoms, and spiritual crises precipitated by the transition. Allow two or three minutes for remembering.

» Remind them that often, when people are grieving, they do not understand that what they are experiencing is normal, so they become frightened. Assuring them they are normal is often the most helpful thing we can do, so it is very important to understand the broad range of grief expressions. Stress the following two points:

1. Grief can happen before a perceived loss (preparatory grief) or after the loss has happened. People with terminal illness deserve the chance to grieve for their own lives, before death.

2. Nearly any physical, mental, emotional, or spiritual symptom may be manifested during grief; there are no rules.

Experiential

» Give them Handout 6, "The Grief Process," asking them to look it over briefly because it explains some of the more common manifestations of grief.

» After about three minutes, ask them to watch the filmstrip, looking for the ways the woman in it deals with her own impending death. Be sure to have tissues in an obvious place, and you might want to have a container of ice water available.

» After the filmstrip, turn on soft instrumental music and quietly break into small groups to share: What were my feelings as I was present to this woman's grief?

» When you end the sharing group, remind them that you will be available this week if any of them want to talk further.

Instruction   » Explain the Grief Energy Cycle, drawing it on the blackboard as you speak. They will be reading about it for homework and will review it next week, so you need to be clear but brief as you explain it now. If you have the film *When A Baby Dies,* you might choose to show the part of it where Nancy Reeves explains this cycle.

Homework   » Assign chapters 4 and 5 in *Grief Ministry* as homework.

» Ask participants to spend some quiet time each day, thinking about the filmstrip and allowing it to touch them in whatever way it will.

» Invite a volunteer to do the opening prayer next session, and show that person a copy of the appropriate section of the session plan.

Closing Prayer   » Join hands and invite participants to share in whatever prayers they feel moved to offer.

» Repeat your offer of support during the week.

Experiencing Pain: Sympathy/Empathy

Purpose To review the Grief Energy Cycle.

To become more sensitive to others' pain.

To understand empathy and sympathy.

Materials

- ☐ Bible and candle
- ☐ Video cassette
  Teach Me To Die
  (or comparable resource)
- ☐ Video cassette player

- ☐ Box of tissues
- ☐ Audio cassette
  (your choice of quiet
  instrumental music)
- ☐ Audio cassette player

- ☐ Blackboard and chalk
- ☐ Copies of the meditation
  "Pictures of Pain"
  (Appendix C)
- ☐ Copies of Handout 8,
  "The Gift of Love"
  (Note that this handout
  comes in both Jewish
  and Christian versions.)

Preparation

- Read to understand Chapter 6 of *Grief Ministry*.
- Set up instrumental music and practice reading meditation.
- Set up the video *Teach Me To Die* or whatever resource you will use.
- Invite one or two people from your faith community who have been grieving for about a year to spend about five minutes each sharing their experiences, especially how they are now experiencing their grief—how far along the journey they have traveled in the past months. Be wise about who you recruit. You want someone who will share deeply (but not take too long) and who will not minimize or deny his/her own pain. If you do not have a suitable person in your community, contact a hospice group or Social Services at a hospital. They likely will be happy to help you locate the right candidate. Prepare your guest to be able to participate in the review of the Grief Energy Cycle later in the session. Including questions from participants, you want this part of the session to only be about fifteen minutes.

Prayer   *Job 16:2-6 or II Corinthians 1:3-6*

» If you choose the first reading, explain a little about the story of Job before you read it. After the reading, invite participants to share on, "Have I ever experienced being 'overwhelmed with speeches' during a time of suffering? What was that like for me?"

» If you choose the second reading, share on, "How have I experienced consolation, from God or people?"

Experiential   *Guest speaker(s) as outlined above. You will likely need to monitor the time closely. This is only one part of the session.*

Instruction   » Review the Grief Energy Cycle, drawing it on the blackboard as you describe it. Ask your guest speakers to tell how this relates to their experience. Remind participants that they should be able to draw this cycle freely in order to help people whenever it is appropriate. This will become one of their most useful tools.

» Explain the difference between empathy and sympathy. (See pages 85 and 86 in *Grief Ministry*.) Invite a few participants to share an experience of having someone "feel sorry for" them and an experience of someone entering into their pain in an empathic way. How did they feel? Explain that sympathy is not a part of good ministry, but ministry without empathy is empty.

Experiential   *Meditation "Pictures of Pain"*

Instruction   » Explain the psychological term "projection."

"Like a movie projector, we project our own feelings onto others. Rather than do this, we need to enter into the experience of others. If we understand our own pain and acknowledge our own need for comfort and support, we will be more able to empathize with others. Projection is a danger in ministry. It makes the minister believe the other person's experience is the same as his/her own and prevents him/her from really hearing the grieving person's needs."

Experiential   » Show the video *Teach Me To Die* or a similar resource that treats the experience of death with gentleness and hope.

In this film, a priest reflects on the death of his mother, hospice workers visit dying people, a coffin maker reflects on his craft.

Homework
» Ask participants to reflect throughout the week on the feelings evoked by today's film and meditation.

» Tell them that if any areas of personal pain open within them, you are available to talk. Prayer and journaling are also helpful.

» Assign Chapter 6 of *Grief Ministry* as reading.

» Give them Handout 8, "The Gift of Love."

» Invite a volunteer to do the opening prayer next session, and show that person the appropriate section of the session plan.

Closing Prayer
» Close with spontaneous shared prayer.

Person-to-Person Skills

Purpose   To learn and experience listening skills.

To deepen awareness of feelings, especially where powerlessness is involved.

Materials

- ☐ Bible and candle
- ☐ Audio cassette player

- ☐ Box of tissues
- ☐ Copies of
  "Group Listening Exercise"
  A or B (Appendix B)
- ☐ Audio cassette
  Listen With Your Heart
  (Deanna Edwards)

- ☐ Filmstrip projector
- ☐ Filmstrip
  Prayer Is Listening
  (Christian groups only)
- ☐ Copies of Handout 9,
  "It Helps To Have
  Friends who Will Listen"

Preparation

- Reread chapters 3 and 6 of *Grief Ministry*.
- Prepare a brief review on feelings (see pages 71-75 of text and materials from Session 2). This time stress the feelings that might surround a person experiencing powerlessness as the result of increasing disability because of illness.
- Prepare a talk on listening skills (pages 75-82 of text).
- Become familiar with whichever Group Listening Exercise you choose (A or B).
- Set up the filmstrip and be sure *Listen With Your Heart* is set at "That's Enough."

Prayer   *I Kings 19:11-13 or John 10:10-11*

These readings show the importance of letting go of preconceived ideas and agendas in order to really listen to and hear another.

» Pray together, asking God to make each person present open to the reality of others, so each will truly be able to listen.

Instruction
» Give the brief review on feelings.

» Talk on listening skills. For Christian groups, show the filmstrip *Prayer Is Listening*. For all groups, stress that when we listen to another we are in communication with God. Listening is a prayerful, creative activity.

» Refer to Chapter 3 in the text and invite participants to tell you what was meaningful for them in that chapter.

Experiential *Group Listening Exercise*

Homework
» Assign Chapters 3 and 6 of *Grief Ministry* as homework reading. Ask them to especially spend time with the "Portrait of a Healing Minister" (pages 89-90), think about each point, and then ask a trusted person how they personally are doing in that area. They should ask someone who will be honest with them, as the point of this exercise is to challenge themselves to grow.

» Give out Handout 9, "It Helps To Have Friends Who Will Listen." Ask participants to simply allow this handout to speak to their hearts as they read.

» Ask participants to be especially aware this week of how they listen to those around them.

» Invite a volunteer to do the opening prayer next session, and show that person a copy of the appropriate section of the session plan.

Closing Prayer
» Play "That's Enough." If you do not have this music, read the words from the front of the textbook in a prayerful way.

» Pray together, asking God to help each person let go of control and really listen as others describe their journeys.

Prayer and Spiritual Resources

Purpose   To learn about and experience both personal prayer and prayer with persons in crisis.

Materials

- ☐ Bible and candle
- ☐ Copies of the song "Someone Who'll Stay" from *Listen With Your Heart* (Appendix C)
- ☐ Copies of Handout 10, "Companions For The Journey"

- ☐ Box of tissues
- ☐ Copies of reflection questions for the reading from "Tobit" (if you choose this reading)
- ☐ Copies of the meditation "God Speaks" (Appendix C)

- ☐ Audio cassette player
- ☐ Audio cassette "Listen With Your Heart" and your choice of instrumental music
- ☐ Copies of "Lemon Exercise" and "Role-playing Exercise" (Appendix B)
- ☐ Bag of lemons (one per participant)

Preparation

- Read and understand chapters 7 and 8 of *Grief Ministry,* and the meditation "God Speaks" (Appendix C).
- Prepare brief talks on prayer as communication (pages 105-107), images of God (pages 97-99, 107-109) and praying with persons in crisis (pages 110-111).
- Become familiar with the two group exercises and the meditation.
- Set up the audio cassette player and make sure *Listen With Your Heart* is set at "Someone Who'll Stay."

Prayer   ***Tobit 5:1-6 or John 10:14-15***

» If you choose the reading from Tobit, explain something about this story (*Grief Ministry*, page 109).

» Explain that Tobit is one of the deuterocanonical books of the Bible, and that although theologians of all faiths have come to respect these books as useful for ministry, they have only been fully accepted by Roman Catholics.

We have chosen this story to illustrate constancy, listening, being the companion of another person on life's journey.

The reading from John was chosen because it illustrates intimacy and presence.

Reflection Questions after Reading Tobit

1. With whom do you identify in this story? Why?

2. Reflect on and describe your own experience of illness, loss, pain, suffering, life threat. Was there someone who was a Raphael (companion) for you at this time? How was that person helpful to you?

3. How did you experience God at that time? What was your prayer like?

Instruction

» Present your talk about prayer. Be sure to stress the importance of coming to prayer "as you are" (text pages 105-107).

» Write on the board some different images of God that are common in our society (e.g., God the Judge, God the Punisher, God the loving parent, God the Aspirin, etc.). Explain how these stereotypical images limit the ability of God to reach both ourselves and others. Invite participants to tell you some images they learned as children and how they relate to God today (text pages 97-99, 107-109).

» Present your brief talk on Praying With Persons in Crisis. It is not necessary to repeat everything in the text, but try to touch on two or three issues that seem important to you. This presentation should only be five minutes at most.

Experiential *Lemon Exercise*

Prayer

» As in Session 4, bring the group to a relaxed, meditative atmosphere. Use soft background music and dim the lights. Prayerfully read the meditation "God Speaks."

» At the end of the meditation, allow the music to play for about three minutes and invite participants to bring their thoughts back to the group when they feel ready.

Experiential *Role Playing Exercise*

Homework

» Assign chapters 7 and 8 in *Grief Ministry* as homework reading.

» Ask them to reflect this week upon whether their prayer flows from, and is applicable to, their daily lived experience. Give them Handout 10 and suggest that they us it for their reflection this week. (If you have not already done so, explain a bit about the story of Tobit.)

» Invite a volunteer to do the Scripture and prayer reflection next week. Show that person the appropriate section in the session outline.

Closing Prayer

» Hand out the words for "Someone Who'll Stay" (Appendix C). Play the song and ask participants to meditate on what the words are saying.

» Invite them to pray silently, asking God to forgive them for times in the past when they have run away from the pain of others and to grace them with courage to abide with those with whom they are called to live and minister.

Depression and Suicide: Trusting Your Pastoral Intuitions

Purpose

» To become aware of pastoral intuitions and responses

» To understand depression and suicide

Materials

- ☐ Bible and candle
- ☐ Copies of the "Scenarios for Discussion" (Appendix B)
- ☐ Box of tissues
- ☐ Copies of Handout 11, "Trusting Your Pastoral Intuitions"
- ☐ Audio cassette player
- ☐ Audio cassette *Listen With Your Heart* (Deanna Edwards)

Preparation

- Reread Chapter 6 and read Chapter 12 of *Grief Ministry*.
- Review sympathy and empathy (text pages 83-89).
- Read Handout 11 and think about the questions that might come up when you read it with the group.
- Prepare a talk on depression and suicide (text pages 159-169).
- Be sure audio cassette is set at the proper place.
- Think about whether you want to give participants a symbol of commissioning (necklace, pin, etc.) and a diploma at the end of the program. Now is the time to shop for these, so you'll be sure to have them in time.

Prayer

Jeremiah 31:3 or II Timothy 1:7

These readings remind us that we can trust our pastoral intuitions because we are empowered by the love and Spirit of God.

» Bring the group to a calm, meditative atmosphere. Suggest that they close their eyes. Invite each person in turn to gently speak aloud one sentence about God in their life. Don't give them too much guidance; let them respond to this request, each in the way right for him/herself. When each has had a chance to speak, thank them and

---

invite them to open their eyes, being aware that they are in God's loving presence.

Instruction

» Review empathy and sympathy. Ask participants to think of a time someone has responded to them with each.

» Together, read Handout 11. This is a time when you will need to trust your own pastoral intuitions, because there is no easy way to explain this concept. You will need to sensitively ask questions of the group until they begin to feel comfortable with the idea. Only experience will really help them to completely understand and "go with the flow" of their own intuitions.

Experiential

» Read aloud the "Scenarios for Discussion." As you read each scenario, ask participants to suggest as many implications as they can, and possible responses. Check whether each response arises more out of sympathy or empathy.

» After the discussion, role-play a couple of the scenarios. Ask participants how they felt in the characters of the scenarios.

Instruction

» Present your talk on depression and suicide. Stress that it is normal to feel guilty when someone we love commits suicide. However, no one person or event can cause another person to want to die. The person's state of mind was caused by the illness of depression, which can be as fatal as many familiar physical illnesses.

Experiential

» Invite participants to share on times they have felt suicidal or have dealt with another person's suicidal death.

Homework

» Ask participants to be open to and attend to whatever feelings arise in them this week. Encourage them to pray about their feelings, reminding them that you (and other staff members) are available if they need to talk during the week.

» Assign chapters 6 and 12 in *Grief Ministry*.

» Invite a volunteer to do the Scripture and prayer reflection next week, and show that person the appropriate section in the session plan.

**Closing
Prayer**

» Play "Walk In The World For Me" (*Listen With Your Heart*). Point out the hope and promise in the song.

» Pray together that you might all be sensitive to those who, because of depression, are walking "in the valley of the shadow" but cannot see the promise of Psalm 23.

Children and Loss: Death of a Baby

Purpose To become sensitive to how children deal with loss.

To address issues around the death of a child/baby or a miscarriage.

Materials
- ☐ Bible and candle
- ☐ Audio cassette player
- ☐ Audio cassette (your choice of soft background music)
- ☐ Box of tissues
- ☐ Copies of Handout 12, "What Good, Then, Is Religion?"
- ☐ Video cassette player
- ☐ Video cassette *When a Baby Dies* (Nancy Reeves)

Preparation
- Read to understand chapters 9 and 10 and pages 153-158 in *Grief Ministry*.
- Make copies of Handout 12.
- Preview film *When a Baby Dies* and set it to begin playing at the part where a mother tells of the death of her child, Jonathan. If you cannot obtain this film, we suggest you invite a couple from your faith community, whose child has died, to share how it has been for them. Choose a couple who have grieved for at least a year, so they will be able to share quite a bit and it will not be unbearably painful for them. Help them prepare their presentation before the session.
- Prepare a talk about the ways children respond to loss and some of the ways an adult might support them (text Chapter 9, and pages 153-158.)

Prayer *Jeremiah 31:15 or Mark 9:36,37*

These readings show how important children are and why the death of a child is so devastating.

To the people of Israel, there was no more poignant illustration of God's love and sorrow when Israel strayed than the picture of a mother weeping for her children. Still today, Jews and Christians see our children as God's and our hope for the future.

Jesus, in using a child for his illustration of love, said, in effect, that caring for a child is caring for God.

Experiential
» Invite participants to share their reflections on the homework reading. They might still have a great heaviness with the pain around suicide; be prepared to give some time here if it is needed.

» Invite each person to tell one way s/he has grown or one important thing s/he has learned so far in the program. This type of feedback helps participants integrate their learning and is good feedback for the facilitator.

Instruction
» Present your talk about how children experience death and loss. It is important to stress that children perceive events differently from adults, and that if a caregiver does not know how a child is thinking, it is advisable to ask the child to tell you about it.

Experiential
» Show the appropriate part of *When A Baby Dies,* or invite your guest couple to speak. This is an emotional time, and you should have lots of tissues handy.

Experiential
» Dim the lights, put on soft background music, and bring the group to a relaxed state with eyes closed. Ask participants to choose one of the following reflections, and to let their minds wander where the reflection leads. Have tissues handy.

> **1. Have I ever lost a young person or baby who was dear to me? At that time, was I helped or hurt by the reactions of those around me?**

Note: We say "lost" here not as a euphemism, but because the loss could happen from divorce or death.

> **2. Imagine that a child I love has died. How do I feel? Who will support me?**

» After about five minutes, invite them to open their eyes and return their attention to the group.

» Move into small groups and spend about five minutes sharing their feelings as they were reflecting.

» Briefly tell participants that you understand that this has been a very emotional session. Remind them that you are available to talk if they need that support during the week. This time is to be spent ministering to participants, making sure they understand that it is fine if they hurt and need nurturing.

Homework

» Assign chapters 9 and 10 and pages 153-158 in *Grief Ministry* as homework reading.

» Ask participants to speak with a child or teenager they know who has experienced a major loss (divorce, death, relocation, etc.) As soon as possible, they should record the interview, adding their own evaluation of how well they communicated with and listened to the child.

» Invite a volunteer to do the opening prayer next session, and show that person a copy of the appropriate section of the session plan.

Closing Prayer

» Together, read Handout 12, "What Good, Then, Is Religion?" This is the conclusion arrived at by one wise person after the death of a child. It may not be the conclusion of all participants and should not be offered as "carved in stone" but as a healthy theology often helpful for ministry.

» Pray together, especially for children around the world who are in pain.

Session 9

Divorce and Other Life Transitions

Purpose   To understand how complicated grief can be when a loss other than death is involved.

Materials

- ☐ Bible and candle
- ☐ Box of tissues
- ☐ Copies of "Scenarios For Role Playing" (Appendix B)

Preparation

- Reread Chapter 4 and read to understand Chapter 11 in *Grief Ministry*.
- Prepare a talk on grief as transition. Mention significant transitions in our society: divorce (because it is so common); relocation (we are so transient, we don't pay enough attention to this grief situation); graduation (every senior has experienced "senioritis"); and twelve-step addiction recovery programs (they require complete restyling of life). Remind them that the grief process means accepting a loss, withdrawing the emotional investment in the object of that loss, and reinvesting in some other relationship or activity. Because this is a complicated process, it takes time. Emphasize that this time is usually longer than they might expect. Speak specifically about divorce as it is presented in the text (Chapter 11), emphasizing the special grief concerns of the grieving and the responses of children.
- Think about the readings you would like to use at the commissioning liturgy in Session 10 so that you will be able to assign readings this week.
- Invite guest speakers from your faith community and help them prepare ten-minute presentations. (This will leave time for each speaker to respond to a couple of questions.) We suggest that you invite an addict who is well into recovery, someone who has been grieving through a divorce, and a third person who has been through a major transition such as relocation or retirement. Invite them to share how the experience has been. Be sure you find speakers who will share openly about their journeys, not people who will say, "I'm fine; it hasn't been at all difficult." Remember, you are trying to help people feel comfortable with the pain of their life transitions; having a speaker who denies all the pain will be counterproductive. You may use Appendix D, "Guest Speaker's Preparation Sheet," if you wish.

Prayer

Ruth 1:15-17 or Luke 2:41-50

If you choose to use the first story, you will want to explain something about the story of Ruth. This is especially important because this story has been popularly applied to celebrations of marriage, and it was not originally intended to be used that way at all. This is the story of two women helping each other through a terrible time of transition.

The second reading tells of a time of transition in the life of Jesus and his family. It is interesting to think how Mary and Joseph must have felt as they saw their child moving away from them, especially at such an early age. What must have been in Jesus' mind as he told his parents he had other things to do, which did not involve them? Did Jesus experience the pain any child feels who must choose a lifestyle different from what parents expect?

» Pray for guidance to be sensitive to the pain of those in the community who are moving through transitions that do not seem important to an observer.

Experiential

» Invite participants to share on their experience interviewing grieving children. Were they nervous? How did they approach the children? How did the children respond? What did they learn?

» Invite them to tell their strongest feelings as they listened to children recounting their pain. Do not be surprised if this experience brought back some childhood memories.

Instruction

» Present your talk on grief as transition.

» Invite your guest speakers to tell their stories. Since you helped them prepare their talks, they will be sharing around some of the concepts taught in this program. Allow each speaker to respond to two or three questions from the group, reminding everyone that there are no simple answers or quick solutions to questions about grief. Tell the speakers to simply respond with what is in their hearts.

Experiential

» Break into small groups and, using the "Scenarios For Role Playing" sheet, role play each scenario. After each role play, ask each player to recount how his/her character felt with the way the story progresses.

Your participants have now developed some strong insights, and you should encourage them to articulate their thoughts and to believe in themselves and depend on their pastoral intuitions.

These are challenging role plays, and if your people can be creative with them, they will feel excited about their potential for real ministry. So give enough time for them to work through the problems, and remember to give plenty of compliments.

Homework

» Assign chapters 4 and 11 in *Grief Ministry*. Ask participants to reread the "Natural Life Transitions" handout from Session 2.

» Tell participants that at the next class they will be asked to evaluate the program. During the week, they might want to think of ways they have grown or ways the program could be improved.

» Invite two volunteers to read at the Commissioning Service next week, and tell them what they will read. Ask each to prepare a five-minute reflection on the reading, as it pertains to what has been learned in this program.

» If you want to have special edible treats for the closing session, you might ask for volunteers to provide "goodies."

Closing Prayer

» Invite participants to stand in a circle with their arms around each other. Encourage them to speak what is in their hearts, in prayer.

Rites and Services: Commissioning Service

Materials

- ☐ Bible
- ☐ Tablecloth and candles; any symbol with meaning for your faith group, to place on the worship table for the liturgy
- ☐ Copies of words for music chosen for commissioning service
- ☐ Optional: Copies of Evaluation Form (Appendix E)

- ☐ Table
- ☐ Four flip charts, hymn books, prayer books, funeral guides, and any other aids for planning funerals within your faith group
- ☐ Copies of order of worship for commissioning service
- ☐ Special treats for break

- ☐ Audio cassette player
- ☐ Audio cassettes of soft music; music chosen for the service; *Listen With Your Heart* (Deanna Edwards)
- ☐ Symbols of commissioning (certificates, necklaces, pins, nametags, etc.)

Preparation

- During the week, think about each participant and pray for wisdom to affirm each in ways that will be meaningful to that person.
- Prepare everything you will need for your commissioning service.
- Be sure *Listen With Your Heart* is set at "Walk In The World For Me." Set any other cassettes where you want them.
- Read to understand Chapter 13 in *Grief Ministry*.
- Think about how you want to receive feedback from participants and prepare evaluation forms if you choose to use them.
- If your pastor or some other official would like to take part in the commissioning service, be sure to extend the invitation, including that person in your planning.

Prayer   *Since the regular Scripture component will be in the commissioning service, a short prayer should begin this session. You might want to express thanks and ask God to guide participants "as we return to the world, to spread the Good News."*

Remind participants about the general numbness of mourners at funerals and memorial services. Ask them about services they have attended. Have they experienced any of the following?

Funerals that seem "canned," where a name was simply fitted into a slot on a page?

Sermons so theoretical that the mourners could not unravel what was being said?

Services that seemed distant and meaningless?

Services that emphasized the hopelessness of death, neglecting the consolation of faith?

Services that only celebrated resurrection and denied the agony of grief?

Services that were intimate and comforting and invited mourners to draw closer to the community of faith?

Experiential

» If there are participants who are involved with planning services at times of death, ask how they attempt to make them relatable and sensitive.

» Divide into four small groups, and ask each group to design a specific service.

Group 1 — This is a funeral for an elderly patriarch whose large family has many mixed feelings. He was mentally and physically abusive to his children but much mellower with his grand- and great-grandchildren. How do you speak to the loving memories of the younger people, while validating the anger of the elders?

Group 2 — A 35-year-old husband and father of four has committed suicide. What can you do and say to help his family grieve?

Group 3 — This is a memorial service one year after the death of a stillborn child. The parents had no memorial ceremony at the time and were advised to pretend it never happened. But they have really been struggling, so you have suggested a service might help.

Group 4 — A 42-year-old woman has died of cancer. She was not ill long and her family (husband and two teenagers) are in shock. You met them only when you were called for funeral preparations. How can you design a service that will reach them and facilitate their grief work?

Optional Group 5 — You might want to add a fifth group to design a funeral for a teenage girl who has died of AIDS. The group should respond to the needs of her parents, who are church members. Stress that it is neither appropriate nor ethical to ask the source of the AIDS infection. However, it is important to be sensitive to the fact that the parents may be dealing with multiple grief because of issues surrounding their daughter's lifestyle.

» Be sure that each group has all aids for funeral design available to your faith group.

» After twenty minutes, bring groups back to the central area, and ask them to report on their planning and explain the reasons why they chose each component of their services. Invite others to comment on each service, and suggest improvements.

Break

We suggest a break here, with some special treats, to celebrate completion of the program. This will allow you to check that your table, diplomas, music and any other needs for the final commissioning service are all set up properly. Bring chairs into a form that reflects the closeness of your group. We prefer circular forms rather than rows of chairs facing the front.

At the end of the break, bring participants to the area you have prepared. You should have quiet music playing in the background.

Evaluation

There are several ways to do this:

» Use the evaluation form included in Appendix E or design your own. If you use a form, give people about fifteen minutes to fill it out right there. If you ask them to fill it out at home, you may not get many back.

» You may prefer to ask participants to spend a few minutes writing you a letter about their growth during the sessions and any suggestions for change in the program.

» You might just invite participants to share aloud how they have grown through this program and if they have any suggestions for changes.

However you do it, be sure to plan time to ask for feedback. You may not be able to implement what they suggest, but they need to be heard. You can make your request for feedback in an upbeat way, not, for example, asking for "beefs and bouquets," or some such format. Suggesting the negative often makes people feel obligated to come up with something wrong. If they have noticed a problem, they'll let you know. If you use words like "change" or "growth" instead of "improvement" or "problem," the evaluation time will have a much more positive atmosphere, people will leave concentrating on the positive, and you will feel better about what you have done.

» Spend no more than twenty minutes on the evaluation.

Homework

» Ask participants to read the rest of the book so they will not miss out on any material, especially Chapter 13, which you dealt with this week.

Commissioning Service

If you have any invited guests for the service, be sure to introduce and welcome them. Coming into a tightly knit group may be difficult for anyone, even a pastor. You might like to allow group members to introduce themselves to the guests.

» Hand out orders of worship and the words to the songs you will play. It is meaningful to meditate on the words as they are sung, and for many people, this is facilitated by having the words in front of them.

» Before asking everyone to listen to the first song, be sure that everyone has finished socializing and is comfortably seated with their attention centered.

» Play "Walk In The World For Me."

» Begin by saying,

> "Today, we are celebrating the end of something, and the beginning of something. We have been meeting here for ten weeks, growing to know each other in ways that nobody has ever known us before. We have learned to be vulnerable to each other, and to trust. We have let go of a lot of old pain, and come to embrace parts of ourselves we hardly knew before.
>
> "I have watched as each of you has grown in self-confidence and ministered to others in the group. I have also noticed the uniquely special qualities of each of you, and now I would like to share that with you."

» Go around the group. Address each person and say something like, "Martha, your specialness for ministry, which I have seen, is your compassionate heart, which cares so much about the pain of others.

> "Freddy, I see your specialness as being a quiet presence to listen when all the rest of the world is rushing around.

"Steve, I'm so glad that you were here, because your honesty in struggling with life helped the rest of us to open up, and I know that your special honesty will help many others you touch through ministry."

» And so on.

First Scripture Reading

» Choose a reading that has been meaningful during the program. As arranged last week, after the reading the reader will share briefly what s/he felt when reading this passage. Or you might ask group members to reflect.

» Play a hymn that is meaningful to your people. The song should reflect a suitable theme, such as God's call or God's abiding love. A good rendition of Psalm 23 would be suitable.

Second Scripture Reading

Same as for First Reading.

Commissioning (by facilitator and invited guests)

» Call each person to the center to be affirmed as especially gifted, anointed on the hands with oil, and to receive some sign of commissioning (a certificate, a necklace, a pin, etc.) and a hug.

Oil is the ancient sign of God's chosen ones and a sign of the people's faith in them as ministers.

» Play a closing song that is meaningful to your group.

Hugs for everyone!!!

To the Facilitator:

Our congratulations are with you! May God bless you for your courage to step out and present a program on such a difficult topic. You are now part of the Grief Ministry family, and if we can ever support you in any way, please let us know.

Love in Christ,

Jo Ann

Donna

Appendix A:
Handouts

The Call to Grief Ministry

To the Facilitator:

We recommend sending the following letter to participants after they register for the program before they come to the first session, or giving it to them at the end of the first session. The margin at the top should allow you to copy it onto your own letterhead.

Dear Participant,

Awareness of God's call may arise within you, like a whispering. Or you may begin to notice that several people make similar comments that they see gifts in you that would be useful to the community. You might see someone else ministering and think, "I'd like to do that, too." However it comes, the initial call can raise all sorts of feelings and questions within you. These questions are healthy and will help you verify that you are called to pastoral ministry within the faith community.

Talk with other people in ministry. Ask them what they have experienced. Encourage them to tell you both the difficulties and the blessings of their choice for ministry, as well as how they deal with their own personal limitations in this area. Let them tell you something of the process of discernment through which they have journeyed.

If you are in this program, you have already received a call. But you are still, in many ways, an unknown quantity for the community. One task of this program is to help you decide the level of commitment you can personally make to pastoral ministry. By the time you complete the ten sessions, you will have a great deal of insight into yourself, your call, and the specific needs of this area of ministry. At the end of the program, you will make a commitment to continuing the ministry in whatever way is right for you and your community.

It is important that you commit to two things. The first commitment we are asking you to make is to yourself and your own integrity. During this program, you will be asked to enter into corners of your own psyche and spirit that you may have closed off, thinking that they were too painful or vulnerable. This may be very difficult, but unless you are willing to challenge yourself in this way, you cannot ask others to allow you to be part of their most intimate life and death experiences. When you closed away those painful areas, it was because you did not know how to cope with the pain they caused you. But now, you are not alone; you have a facilitator with skills to help you examine and journey through those painful valleys of your life. And you have a peer group that will completely respect and support you in your journey. That makes a big

Grief Ministry Facilitator's Guide
© 1992 Resource Publications, Inc.

Handout 1

difference. Now it is up to you to move forward in trust, challenging yourself to honesty and personal integrity.

You don't have to worry now about what this may mean. As the program unfolds, you will have many chances to allow it to touch you in vulnerable places. Each time, the choice will be up to you: "Will I allow myself to hurt in order to grow, or will I choose to keep this area of my life closed?" There is no right answer; only you will know what you are ready to share or examine at that moment.

The other commitment we ask you to make is to the group. Just as you will challenge yourself to personal honesty and growth, each member of the group will do the same. Each of them will experience nervousness and pain. Each will wonder if you can be trusted to receive and cherish their experiences when they share openly. Only if they trust you will they feel able to accept the challenge to be open and honest.

It is vitally important to the dynamic of this program that you commit to absolute confidentiality. In the future, there will be times when you are tempted to share with other people what went on in the group. You must know that this is never acceptable.

Your ability to accept the limitations and responsibilities of confidentiality is one measure of your suitability for this ministry. Once you are used to the idea, you will realize that it also allows you to share personally in the security of knowing that your thoughts and struggles will not be spread around the larger community. So right now, make this commitment.

Finally, after each session, allow yourself a few minutes to examine your larger commitment to this ministry. Is that commitment changing, in its depth or in your insights about what it involves? This ongoing process will allow you, at the end of the program, to realistically evaluate your own commitment and to move into active ministry with your eyes open. This, too, is a matter of personal integrity.

Through this ministry you will likely find deeper satisfaction and receive richer love than you can imagine now. To be invited to share moments of agony and triumph with another human being is one of the most beautiful gifts we can receive. Relax and enjoy your ministry, knowing that God is with you.

Signed,

Death Inventory

Circle the number that best speaks for your reaction to the statements, with 5 standing for strong agreement and 1 standing for strong disagreement.

1. I hardly ever think of death.   1 2 3 4 5

2. I wish that life would not fly by so fast.   1 2 3 4 5

3. I hate the thought of looking at a dead body.   1 2 3 4 5

4. I think pre-planning funerals is ghoulish.   1 2 3 4 5

5. I am afraid of having a fatal illness.   1 2 3 4 5

6. I change the subject when people talk about death.   1 2 3 4 5

7. I think it is important to visit friends
who are very ill in the hospital.   1 2 3 4 5

8. I worry about being in a nursing home someday.   1 2 3 4 5

9. If the person I love most dies, I will have a hard
time going on with life.   1 2 3 4 5

Answer these questions honestly:

What do I believe about heaven and hell?

What does the word 'resurrection' mean to me?

Grief Ministry Facilitator's Guide
© 1992 Resource Publications, Inc.

If I were planning my funeral, what would be important to me?

If this were the last day of my life, with whom would I want to speak? What would I want to say?

What have I learned about myself from the above answers?

Natural Life Transitions

Birth — leaving the safety of the womb for the unfamiliar world.

Beginning school — leaving the security of home/parent(s), for a world full of strangers, different social patterns.

Graduation — from each school level to another level where there are more people and different/more mature behavior is expected.

Graduation from high school or university into the "adult" world means leaving childhood behind. Often, reunions are times when normally mature adults resort to childish behavior patterns.

Moving to a new house/city/country — new environment, friendships, cultural patterns, demanding adaptation.

Marriage — demands new behaviors sometimes interpreted as loss of freedom, self, independence.

Loss of employment, through being fired, laid off, or retired — The retirement period is the highest time of suicide among American males. Loss of employment or "what you do" is often experienced as "loss of who you are."

Major or chronic illness — loss of independence and control over body and life. Control may fall into the hands of medical people or of the disease itself.

Loss of limb through amputation — requires a new self-definition and may mean a loss of mobility, independent functioning.

Natural aging process — often means that a person becomes physically less able and must rely on others for functions previously performed independently.

Stroke — This is a disease, but since the reality of the stroke patient's loss is so strong, we have included it as a special class.

Moving from one's adult home to a retirement home, the home of a child, or a nursing home — All control seems to pass into the hands of other people.

Grief Ministry Facilitator's Guide
© 1992 Resource Publications, Inc.

Loss of a significant other through death — means that a person must completely redefine the parameters of life. This significant other may be a pet.

Divorce — Effects upon adults and children are different, but equally devastating.

Loss of grandchildren because of custodial battles between parents — Often, grandparents' pain is not considered.

Loss of credibility — As people in our society grow older, we tend not to consider their wisdom and experience but to treat them as people "past their prime," and to put them "out to pasture." This creates alienation and frustration.

Loss of physical beauty as it is worshiped in our society — We see late middle-aged persons trying to disguise the natural aging process with makeup, clothing, exercise, tanning, etc. Loss of physique is perceived as loss of personal value.

Loss of supervisory person through transfer — evident when a beloved minister or priest moves from a church. People may have a hard time accepting the new person, not because they are rejecting the replacement but because they are grieving the one who has left. This also happens in supervisory employment positions and with step-parents. If these losses are understood, patience will often pay off.

Loss of financial independence — Self-identity as an adult is often tied to the ability to "look after" oneself financially.

Loss of a baby through abortion (spontaneous or therapeutic) or miscarriage — Often, this loss is denied, and necessary grief work not accomplished. This can have very serious ramifications in future relationships.

Birth of a child perceived as "imperfect" — This may be the birth of a handicapped child, when parents must grieve for the idealized child that "existed" in their minds before the birth. Or it may be the birth and development of a normal, average child to parents who are high achievers or who need to achieve vicariously through their children.

The journey of recovery from an addiction through the twelve steps — is like being born again. It may mean completely changing peer groups, even jobs. Friends associated with the addictive behavior are usually not supportive of the addict who enters a recovery program. And there is the usual grieving for the "best friend," the drug of choice.

Grief Ministry Facilitator's Guide
© 1992 Resource Publications, Inc.

The spouse of a person recovering from addictions must grieve for the familiar patterns of the dysfunctional life nurtured by the addict. While this person may be happy to change, it means developing new parameters for the relationship.

The Life Continuum

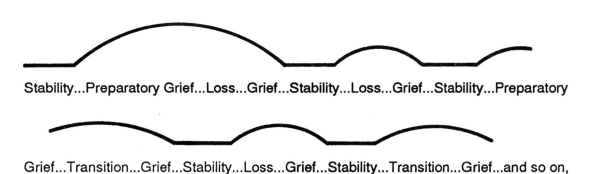

Stability...Preparatory Grief...Loss...Grief...Stability...Loss...Grief...Stability...Preparatory

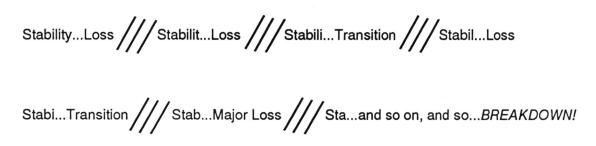

Grief...Transition...Grief...Stability...Loss...Grief...Stability...Transition...Grief...and so on,

and so on, and so on...

The periods of stability are really plateaux between transitions and losses (large or small). If we have a chance to experience preparatory grief before a loss or transition, the grief afterward will be diminished. The grief periods provide psycho/spiritual "bridges" between trauma and stability. However, if those bridges are never built through grief work, walls will be built instead, and the stability that follows will be diminished.

Stability...Loss /// Stabilit...Loss /// Stabili...Transition /// Stabil...Loss

Stabi...Transition /// Stab...Major Loss /// Sta...and so on, and so...*BREAKDOWN!*

The bridges become walls. Each grief becomes more deeply buried and harder to express. Less and less of the person's wholeness can move past each wall. More pain festers within the psyche and spirit with each unexpressed grief.

Thoughts or Feelings?

A feeling is an emotion. It may have physical symptoms such as sweaty palms when frightened or tears when angry. Each person has his/her own set of physical signs that tell how s/he is feeling. One woman says, "I must be worrying, because I feel like I have a tight band around my head." Another person tells us, "I eat all my tension and anger, and then I get an upset stomach."

Often, it is difficult to decide whether you are relating to the environment through the intellect or through the emotions.

Society teaches us not to show certain emotions that are considered "bad" or "weak." So if John becomes angry when his marriage ends, he will likely try to push away that anger and do something to keep his mind off his feelings.

But feelings do not go away. They just build up inside like a time bomb waiting to explode. It becomes essential for emotional, physical, and spiritual health to learn to identify, name, and validate all feelings. Brutal honesty with yourself is, in this case, the most healthy route.

Ministers to the grieving help other people understand their feelings too. Some of these may have been pushed away and denied for such a long time that they are nearly unrecognizable, especially to their owners.

There is a rule of thumb that often will help you decide if a statement with the word "feel" in it is really a statement of intellect or thought. <u>If you can put the word "that" after the word "feel," then the person is not stating a feeling but an idea or thought.</u>

For example, someone says to you, "I feel I shouldn't be here." Into that sentence place the word "that": "I feel that I shouldn't be here." This sentence is clearly a statement of a judgment, not a feeling. Help the person articulate the reasons for the judgment.

Note that feelings may be connected to this judgment. Is the person afraid, nervous, angry? Is this why she made the statement using the word "feel?" If you can help the person name and

© 1992 Resource Publications, Inc.

understand the emotions s/he feels in this situation, s/he may no longer have a need to leave. His/her judgment may change.

Unidentified feelings are uncontrolled feelings, and they can often take control of a person's actions. Naming them allows the person to resume control and make valid decisions. So, it is important that we as ministers know how to help people understand the feelings behind their judgments. Then they can change their "that" statements, which they thought were expressing their true feelings, into real feeling statements.

In order to help you better recognize a feeling statement and separate feelings from thoughts, complete this exercise.

1. Are these feeling or thought statements?

"I feel John is too young to die."

"I feel like running away."

"John feels there are too many children in the world."

"I feel as if my world is spinning too fast."

"I feel I don't want to go to the hospital!"

2. For each of the above statements, look for the opposite implication.

For example, "I feel I don't want to go to the hospital," is obviously a statement of thought or judgment. If you asked the person, "Why don't you want to go?" he would be likely to reply, "Because I don't. I just don't."

But if you wonder to yourself, "What might be the feeling implication of that thought statement?" you might then ask, "Mr. Smith, how does it make you feel when someone suggests that you go to the hospital?" Or, "Mr. Smith, have you ever had a bad experience with hospitals? Does the thought of going to the hospital bring up some strong feeling or memory for you?

This sort of question makes the person feel validated, as if you really want to know about his reasons. You are not just another person here to persuade him to do something he doesn't want. It can also open doors for him to begin to understand his own response and to learn if his unidentified feelings have been controlling his judgments.

Similarly, if a person speaks a feeling such as, "I feel so lonely here," you can ask yourself, "What is the judgment behind that loneliness?" The interested minister might ask, "Mrs. Potter, have you felt lonely a lot in your life, or is this a feeling you have more now that your daughter has died?" Or you might say, "Loneliness is a very hard feeling to have because sometimes when we feel lonely, we think nobody else even cares. Is that what you think when you feel lonely?"

Remember, we are not called to take away the other person's feelings, or to make things better. But often when people meet someone who is genuinely interested in understanding them and who demonstrates that interest in a skillful way, their self-image takes a turn upward and their burdens seem a bit lighter.

The Grief Process

Grief is the emotional, physical, and spiritual reaction to the loss (or perceived loss) of someone (or something) in whom (or which) one has been deeply emotionally invested.

Grieving *must happen*. It is the natural healing process in emotional loss. If it is not facilitated at the appropriate time, it will be retained (repressed) within the person and will surface at some later stage, often as depression.

The sooner after the loss that grief work is done, the more effective will be the healing and readaptation to life.

Most of us are grieving, most of the time, for some implication of our life. The acknowledgment of that reality is part of healthy maturity.

Grief takes longer than we expect. A major loss, such as the death of a family member, or divorce, will likely take three to five years.

Preparatory grief happens before the actual loss, when the person perceives that an unavoidable loss is approaching. Preparatory grief has the same dynamics as grief after the loss, and if this happens, grief after the loss may be appreciably shorter in duration.

Grief Milestones

Acute Milestones

Numbness — may seem as if life is on television, happening in front of the person, who is not personally involved.

Denial — "If I deny the reality, perhaps it will go away."

These reactions are the human psyche's natural response to a situation too big to handle all at once. The person needs to be respected and reassured that s/he is normal and that the caregiver will be there to help whenever the person is ready to move on.

Transitional Milestones

Anger — "I can no longer deny the reality of what is happening, but I can try to fight back."

Bargaining — "Maybe I can strike a bargain to get some power figure to change the reality."

Guilt — "If I can find something that I did to cause the loss, maybe I can reverse the process." This is the "If only..." moment.

The problem with these reactions is that usually there is not an appropriate focus. I can sue the person whom I perceive as causing my loss, but I will still feel empty inside. I can shout at the physician who diagnosed my cancer, but the cancer will not respond to my shouting. I can try to be a good patient, bargaining with the healthcare givers so they will make me better, but my emphysema will not go away.

Sometimes we are surprised to hear normally stable people venting all sorts of inappropriate guilt feelings, and we may try to reassure them that they did not cause the loss. But we must remember that such self-searching is part of the normal process.

Recovery Milestones

Depression — This is the natural reaction to accepting the reality that an unpleasant situation cannot be changed.

Peace and Acceptance — The person comes to the point of being able to live comfortably with the reality. He has withdrawn emotional investment in the lost life parameters, feels whole again, and is ready to reinvest in new relationships and activities.

When the grieving person becomes depressed, many people do not recognize this as progress, and become worried. They try to cheer up the person. In reality, the griever needs to be told, "I can understand why you feel so down. I feel terrible too, that you're going to die (have lost your job/husband/etc.). It's natural to feel depressed at a time like this. But we'll get through this together." Don't try to own the other person's pain or take it away; acknowledge it and offer support.

Note: All of the above presumes that the grief process is taking place in a normally healthy psyche. If there is a state of emotional unhealthiness, then grieving will likely also have unhealthy manifestations, and professional help will be needed. Do not be afraid to ask for advice from a professional grief counselor. Even if s/he only reassures you that all is well, you will feel better.

The Use of Energy While Grieving

Below is a diagram helpful to people after a loss (e.g., parent(s) who, after the death of a child, are deciding when to conceive another; or any other major life transition). This is based on the places where people are using their energy. (Used courtesy of Nancy Reeves, Ph.D.)

Energy = force that allows you to be, do, think...

The three places where people use energy are Grieving Readjustment (GR), Survival (S), and Life Enhancement (LE). The following shows the various phases people experience after a loss. If not in the fourth stage, energy must come from survival, and this presents problems.

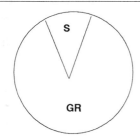

1. Survival functions—plodding along, unaware

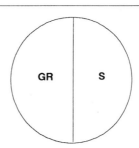

2. Person able to do what needs to be done in order to exist. "I feel worse now." Person may feel worse because of awareness of what's happening.

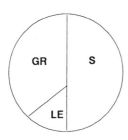

3. "I feel lighter. It's easier." More interest, fulfillment in what they're doing. Make choices, reach out to others, find a hobby.

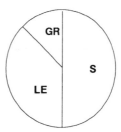

4. Can't wipe out grieving entirely, or else memory of the mourned person is wiped out. Grief doesn't restrict the person, except that anniversaries, etc., will put them into more grieving.

© 1992 Resource Publications, Inc.

The Gift of Love
(Jewish Version)

When we hear the word "ministry," we generally think of a particular formalized type of service done by the rabbi or one of the people who assist with formal worship. Or we might think of individuals who have used their unique gifts to help others (like musician, puppeteer, or teacher).

Into every community of believers, God will send people of many talents: some to touch and preach, some to dream and envision, some to lead in worship, some to nurture and create. God, who is completely good, will send to the faith community the right people for their sustenance and growth.

Most of us don't think that we might be special enough to really minister. Our talents seem so ordinary.

But there is a special ministry that can be of rich benefit to everyone whose life we touch. We call it the ministry of listening.

Webster's Dictionary defines the word "listen" as "to pay attention to sound; to hear with thoughtful attention; to be alert to catch an unexpected sound."

How many of us *really* listen to others? We're so wrapped up in ourselves, our own thoughts and feelings, that the words and feelings of others pass by unheard and not even recognized. Truly, in one ear and out the other.

Listening. Easier said than done! Some call it an art. Others say it is a skill, which can be improved with practice just like reading, writing and speaking.

Skill or art, it isn't easy. It takes much effort to be a good listener, just as it does to be a good speaker. You must learn to listen with more than the ears. Silent body language—your eyes, facial expressions, posture, and gestures—often communicates more than voice or words.

Listening is active, not passive. You can't just sit there like the proverbial bump on a log. Most of all, good listening involves your attitude. If you have respect and reverence for others, it shows in the way you listen to them.

Test your listening skills by answering these questions.

1. Do I show genuine interest in the other person, encouraging him/her to talk?

2. Do I look at the other person?

3. Do I try to block out distractions around me?

4. Does my body language encourage the person who is speaking (smile, nod, etc.)?

5. Am I aware of his/her body language (expressions, posture, gestures), which may help me understand his/her words?

6. Am I *thinking* about what this person is saying?

7. Do I consider *why* the person is saying what s/he is?

8. Do I try to avoid judging?

9. Am I really listening, or am I trying to anticipate what s/he will say?

10. Do I let him/her finish, encouraging him/her to continue if s/he hesitates?

11. If s/he becomes emotional, do I remain calm without being detached from his/her emotions?

12. Do I ask questions if I'm not sure I fully understand?

13. Do I resist giving answers, opinions, and advice, instead letting the other person talk it out and come to his/her own conclusions?

14. Do I give my *full* attention to what s/he is saying, or am I thinking about what I will say in response?

The psalms are full of invocations to a God who will save and heal the people. The psalmist tells us with great assurance, "Yahweh listens when I call to him" (Psalm 4:3b). When Israel was in slavery in Egypt, the people cried out in their misery, and God said,

> I have heard the groaning of the Israelites, enslaved by the Egyptians, and have remembered my covenant. I shall redeem you with outstretched arm; I shall take you as my people and I shall be your God (Exodus 6:5-7).

God promised to heal the nation and to reward the faithful people. God honored Solomon's Temple as the house of holy sacrifice, and told Solomon that:

> ...if my people who bear my name humble themselves, and pray and seek my presence and turn from their wicked ways, then I will listen from heaven, and forgive their sins and

restore their country. Now and for the future my eyes are open and my ears attentive to prayer offered in this place (II Chronicles 7:14,15).

Today, we cannot offer sacrifice at Solomon's temple, and often it is only through our presence that God will be manifested to another hurting human being. It is interesting that God said, "Now my eyes will be open and my ears attentive...." How many of us listened *attentively,* with our ears and our eyes, to our children or our spouses or colleagues, when they needed to speak with us recently? God is our model for life, and God is a completely interested listener.

> I am filled with love when Yahweh listens
> to the sound of my prayer,
> when he bends down to hear me,
> as I call (Psalm 116:1-2).

People need to be listened to. This is a basic need common to all. We need to share ideas, attitudes, feelings, fears, desires. In order to share these, there has to be someone to listen. The better the listener, the deeper the communication. We are constantly bombarded by words from all sides, either being talked *at* or *to.* A good listener is a rare friend, who by listening is saying, "You are wonderful, and what you have to say is important."

The greatest benefit of our listening ministry is to help another person receive healing. We may have other important things to do, but if we stop and listen to someone who needs to talk, we are imitating God, the supreme healer, who always has time to listen to us.

> Give ear to my words, Yahweh,
> spare a thought for my sighing.
> Listen to my cry for help,
> my King and my God!
>
> To you I pray, Yahweh,
> At daybreak you hear my voice;
> at daybreak I lay my case before you
> and fix my eyes on you (Psalm 5:1-3).

Listening is a gift of love you can give no matter who you are or where you are, and you can give it to anyone. It is especially important to your family, but every day you will meet others who need this gift.

This gift is needed now. It is a natural gift that God has given to each of us for the support of other people. Most of us have forgotten how to use the natural gifts of our eyes, ears, and attention. Let us decide today that at the next opportunity, we will try to listen well and to support and comfort others for the glory of God.

With thanks to Rev. William Rabior, "Five Ministries For Your Everyday Life," *Liguorian Magazine,* Liguori, Missouri 63057 (February 1983).

The Gift of Love (Christian Version)

When we hear the word "ministry," we generally think of a particular type of formalized service done by ordained persons or by lay people at community worship. Or we might think of certain individuals who have used their unique gifts in service to others (such as puppet ministry, teaching, or music ministry. The apostle Paul tells us:

> There are many different gifts but it is always the same Spirit; there are many different ways of serving, but it is always the same Lord. There are many different forms of activity, but in everybody it is the same God who is at work in them all. The particular manifestation of the Spirit granted to each one is to be used for the general good (I Corinthians 12:4-7).

We would like to share with you a kind of ministry open to all. We call it the ministry of listening.

Webster's Dictionary defines the word "listen" as "to pay attention to sound; to hear with thoughtful attention; to be alert to catching an unexpected sound."

How many of us *really* listen to others? We're so wrapped up in ourselves, our own thoughts and feelings, always ready to defend our own ideas, that the words and feelings of others pass by unheard and not even recognized. Truly, in one ear and out the other.

Listening. Easier said than done! Some call it an art. Others say it is a skill, which can be improved with practice just like reading, writing, and speaking. It takes effort to be a good listener, just as it takes to be a good speaker. A good listener learns to listen with more than the ears. Silent body language—your eyes, facial expressions, posture, and gestures—often communicates more than voice or words.

Listening is active, not passive. You can't just sit there like the proverbial bump on a log. Most of all, good listening involves your attitude. If you have respect and reverence for others, it shows in the way you listen to them.

Test your listening skills by answering these questions.

1. Do I show genuine interest in the other person, encouraging him/her to talk?

2. Do I look at the other person?

3. Do I try to block out distractions around me?

4. Does my body language encourage the person who is speaking (smile, nod, etc.)?

5. Am I aware of his/her body language (expressions, posture, gestures), which may help me understand his/her words?

6. Am I *thinking* about what this person is saying?

7. Do I consider *why* the person is saying what s/he is?

8. Do I try to avoid judging?

9. Am I really listening, or am I trying to anticipate what s/he will say?

10. Do I let him/her finish, encouraging him/her to continue if s/he hesitates?

11. If s/he becomes emotional, do I remain calm without being detached from his/her emotions?

12. Do I ask questions if I'm not sure I fully understand?

13. Do I resist giving answers, opinions, and advice, instead letting the other person talk it out and come to his/her own conclusions?

14. Do I give my *full* attention to what s/he is saying, or am I thinking about what I will say in response?

Jesus has all the qualities of a good listener. We can follow his example. Jesus was/is a(n):

creative listener — he asked questions, gave new insights and new ways of looking at a situation.

sensitive listener — he felt *for* others, read their body language well.

empathic listener — he felt *with* others, and showed his feelings with a touch, a word of affirmation, an understanding look.

non-judgmental listener — he did not judge, but found meaning in the lives of those he met.

Read and reflect on these Scripture passages for a sampling of how Jesus listened and responded: Luke 22:24-27, Luke 19:1-10, Luke 7:36-50.

> I am filled with love when Yahweh listens
> to the sound of my prayer,
> when he bends down to hear me,
> as I call (Psalm 116:1-2).

People need to be listened to. This is a basic need common to all. We need to share ideas, attitudes, feelings, fears, desires. In order to share these, there has to be someone to listen. The better the listener, the deeper the communication. We are constantly bombarded with words from all sides, being talked *at* or *to*. Not often do we find someone who truly wants to listen. A good listener is a rare friend, who by listening is saying, "You are worthwhile, and what you have to say is important."

The greatest benefit of our listening ministry is to help another person receive healing. We may have other important things to do, but if we stop and listen to someone who needs to talk, we are acting in imitation of Christ, the great listening healer.

> Give ear to my words, Yahweh,
> spare a thought for my sighing.
> Listen to my cry for help,
> my King and my God!
>
> To you I pray, Yahweh.
> At daybreak you hear my voice;
> at daybreak I lay my case before you
> and fix my eyes on you (Psalm 5:2).

Listening is a gift of love you can give no matter who you are or where you are, and you can give it to anyone. It is especially important to your family, but every day you will meet others who need this gift.

Your gift is needed now. It is a natural gift that God has given to each of us for the support of others. Most of us have forgotten how to use the natural gifts of our eyes, ears, and attention. Let us decide today that at the next opportunity, we will try to listen well and to support and comfort others for the glory of God.

With thanks to Rev. William Rabior, "Five Ministries For Your Everyday Life," *Liguorian Magazine*, Liguori, Missouri 63057 (February 1983).

© 1992 Resource Publications, Inc.

It Helps to Have Friends Who Will Listen

When I ask you to listen to me and you start giving me advice, you have not done what I asked.

When I ask you to listen to me and you begin to tell me why I shouldn't feel that way, you are trampling on my feelings.

When I ask you to listen to me and you feel you have to do something to solve my problems, you have failed me, strange as that may seem.

Listen! All I asked was that you listen, not talk or do—just hear me.

Advice is cheap; twenty-five cents will get you both Dear Abbey and Billy Graham in the same newspaper.

And I can do for myself. I'm not helpless. Maybe discouraged and faltering, but not helpless.

When you do something for me that I can and need to do for myself, you contribute to my fear and inadequacy.

But when you accept as a simple fact that I do feel what I feel, no matter how irrational, then I can quit trying to convince you and get behind this business of understanding what's behind the irrational feeling.

And when that's clear, the answers are obvious and I don't need advice. Irrational feelings make sense when we understand what's behind them.

Perhaps that's why prayer works, sometimes, for some people...because God is mute and doesn't give advice or try to fix things.

God just listens and lets you try to work it out for yourself.

So please listen and just hear me.

And if you want to talk, wait a minute for your turn...and I'll listen to you.

Author unknown.

Companions for the Journey

Am I willing to suffer with the people here, the suffering of the powerless, the feeling impotent? Can I say to my neighbors, "I have no solutions. I don't know the answers. But I will work with you, search with you, be with you"? (Sr. Ita Ford, M.M., shortly before her death at the hands of soldiers in El Salvador.)

A Companion For The Journey:

Then Tobias answered him, "Father, I will do everything that you have commanded me; but how can I obtain the money when I do not know the man?" Then Tobit gave him the receipt and said to him, "Find a man to go with you and I will pay him wages as long as I live; and go and get the money." So, he went to look for a man and he found Raphael, who was an angel, but Tobias did not know it. Tobias said to him, "Can you come with me to Media? Are you acquainted with that region?" The angel replied, "I will journey with you; I am familiar with the road" (Tobit 5:1-6).

Reflection Questions

1. What was Sr. Ita asking of herself in her question? If you personally respond to her invitation, what commitment will that entail?

2. Has someone ever demonstrated a commitment to journey with you through a painful time? Was the companionship helpful?

3. We are seldom asked to actually die for others as Sr. Ita did. But your commitment likely means that you will give up something. What are you willing to give? (There are no right or wrong answers; this is simply a time to examine insights about your own choices.)

4. Could you "angel" a frightened traveler as Raphael did, all the while knowing that you had no easy answers as Sr. Ita stated?

Grief Ministry Facilitator's Guide
© 1992 Resource Publications, Inc.

Trusting Your Pastoral Intuitions

An important aspect of your presence and ministry to others lies in learning to trust yourself and the intuitions that come from within you. You can learn to become more aware of your inner "hunches" or messages, which help you understand and empathize with the experiences of those around you. These are pastoral intuitions.

When you are with another, try to listen with a "double attentiveness." You listen to the other person and pay attention to the person and the situation, but you also listen to what you are feeling in yourself. You will get an inner sense of what seems to be the most helpful thing to say or do in this particular situation.

Another way to develop your intuitive skills is to really tune into non-verbal communication. Learn to attend carefully to the message conveyed by body stance and tone of voice. Then, you can begin to intuit the possible meanings of those communications. Of course, you can always check out what you think you are finding. You might say something like, "John, you're telling me that everything is fine, but I see you pacing the room, and I find that your eyes never meet mine. That leads me to think maybe there's more to the situation than you're saying. I don't want to pry, but perhaps it would help you if someone listened to what's worrying you." Remember to be aware of what your own non-verbal communication is saying!

Your intuitions may seem like thoughts coming from within and through your head. Some people experience them as a small voice giving ideas and warnings. Others have said that they experience their intuitions as "the voice of God, guiding and giving insight and wisdom."

I (DRW) will sometimes have a flash or a thought that is completely surprising and causes me to change the outline of a day of reflection or a retreat. The flash tells me that someone in the group has a certain need that I did not anticipate when I was planning the outline. It may come because of a person's sharing, or just because I pick up certain vibrations that let me know I need to pay close attention and be open and flexible. It is hard to describe. But

I have learned to listen, and I believe it is the Holy Spirit guiding me when my human insights are limited.

In other pastoral situations, I will have a thought like "Something is wrong here" or "There's more to this situation than meets the eye." Often, I will not be sure why my intuition is giving me this thought, but again, I have learned to be watchful and flexible and to ask the kind of questions that bring deeper insights.

One professional minister whom I respect has told me that when things are going badly, he gets itchy. It sounds strange, but he trusts his itches. Somehow, his body has learned that to make him attend to intuitive messages, it has to give him a physical message. Perhaps this is why so many people scratch their heads when they stop to think!

Paying attention to your intuitions is hard to do if you have not been accustomed to valuing your inner experiences and hunches. There is so much in our society that invites and attracts people to pay more attention to material and exterior realities—and to place trust and confidence in them. So you may need to shift gears, learn to believe in what wells up inside you, and to act upon it.

Sometimes there might be interferences in your inner messages because of past painful experiences. For example, if you had a dominating father, you may receive messages from your feelings not to trust males in authority positions. Or, if you lived your childhood in fear of not measuring up to the expectations of siginificant adults, you may still fear that what you say and do is not good enough; thus you may hesitate to trust your intuitions. Most adults have some interferences such as these. As you become aware of them, it is possible to be healed of the pain that causes them.

Some persons are more naturally attentive to physical and exterior things, but everyone has intuitions and can become more aware of this part of themselves. To grow in developing and using your intuitions, you need to pay attention to and listen to the feelings and bodily sensations that are stirring within you, and try to put words on this inner experience. The more that you listen and act on them, the more you will develop this part of yourself. It is comparable to the physician who gets better at diagnosing an illness after s/he has seen its symptoms several times. As you deal with more and more pastoral situations, you will learn to be insightful about what is below the surface; thus you will be able to support others more deeply.

© 1992 Resource Publications, Inc.

What Good, Then, Is Religion?

In a sense, I have been writing this book for fifteen years. From the day I heard the word "progeria" and was told what it meant, I knew that I would one day have to face [my son] Aaron's declining and dying. And I knew that after he died, I would feel the need to write a book, sharing with others the story of how we managed to go on believing in God and in the world after we had been hurt. I didn't know what I would call the book, and I wasn't totally sure what I would say. But I knew that the page after the title page would carry a dedication to Aaron. I could visualize the dedication to him, and under it, in my mind's eye, I could see the quotation from the Bible, the words of King David after the death of his son: "Absolom, my son! Would that I had died instead of you!"

Then one day, a year and a half after Aaron's death, I realized that I was visualizing the page differently in my imagination. Now instead of the passage in which David wishes he were dead and his son alive, I saw in my mind's eye the words of David after the death of an earlier child, the passage that I have in fact used in part on the dedication page of this book:

> When David saw the servants whispering, he said to them, Is the child dead? And they said, He is dead. And David rose and washed and changed his clothing and asked that food be set before him, and he ate. The servants said to him, What is this that you are doing? You fasted and wept for the child when he was alive, and now that he is dead, you get up and eat! And David said: While the child was yet alive, I fasted and wept, for I said, Who knows whether the Lord will be gracious to me, and the child will live. But now that he is dead, why should I fast? Can I bring him back again? I shall go to him, but he will not return to me (II Samuel 12:19-23).

I knew then that the time had come for me to write my book. I had gone beyond self-pity to the point of facing and accepting my son's death. A book telling people how much I hurt would not do anyone any good. This had to be a book that would affirm life. It would have to say that no one ever promised us a life free from pain and disappointment. The most anyone promised us was that we would not be alone in our pain, and that we would be able to draw upon a source outside ourselves for the strength and courage we would need to survive life's tragedies and life's unfairness.

I am a more sensitive person, a more effective pastor, a more sympathetic counselor because of Aaron's life and death than I would ever have been without it. And I would give up all of those gains in a second if I could have my son back. If I could choose, I would forego all the spiritual growth and depth that has come my way because of our experiences, and be what I was fifteen years ago, an average rabbi, an indifferent counselor, helping some people and unable to help others, the father of a bright, happy boy. But I cannot choose.

I believe in God. But I do not believe the same things about Him that I did years ago, when I was growing up or when I was a theological student. I recognize His limitations. He is limited in what He can do by laws of nature and by the evolution of human nature and human moral freedom. I no longer hold God responsible for illness, accidents and natural disasters, because I realize that I gain little and I lose so much when I blame God for those things. I can worship a God who hates suffering, but cannot eliminate it, more easily than I can worship a God who chooses to make children suffer and die, for whatever exalted reason. Some years ago, when the "death of God" theology was a fad, I remember seeing a bumper sticker that read, "My God is not dead; sorry about yours." I guess my bumper sticker reads, "My God is not cruel; sorry about yours."

God does not cause our misfortunes. Some are caused by bad luck, some are caused by bad people, and some are simply the inevitable consequences of our being human and being mortal, living in a world of inflexible natural laws. The painful things that happen to us are not punishment for our misbehavior, nor are they in any way part of some grand design on God's part. Because the tragedy is not God's will, we need not feel hurt or betrayed by God when tragedy strikes. We can turn to Him for help in overcoming it, precisely because we can tell ourselves that God is as outraged by it as we are.

---

1. Harold S. Kuschner, *When Bad Things Happen to Good People* (New York: Random House, Inc.), 1981.

Appendix B:
Exercises

Exercise 1

Group Listening Exercise (A)

It is very important to stress to all participants that this is an exercise, not a time for idle chatter. The observers are to sit in absolute silence as if they were not part of the group. From experience, we know that if you do not stress this, things can rapidly deteriorate.

1. Divide participants into groups of three. Do not create a "leftover" group of two. Put them, instead, into two other groups.

2. Ask one person from each group to leave the room.

3. Choose one person from each group to be the interviewer, and the other will be the observer.

4. The interviewer will ask the person who is presently out of the room all about his/her life and interests. The interviewer will attempt to establish eye contact and reflect complete interest in every possible way, making the person feel completely validated.

5. The observer will watch and report to the group.

6. Invite the absent people back to their groups and tell them that they will be interviewed so that the interviewer can practice good listening skills.

7. Allow five minutes for the interview.

8. After the interview, ask the reporters to tell what they observed.

9. Ask the persons who were interviewed how the experience was for them.

10. Send a different person from each group out of the room.

11. Choose a new interviewer from each group. Make sure the observers from the first part of the exercise have a more active role this time. The other member of the groups will be observers.

12. Repeat the instructions from the first part. However, at a signal from you (perhaps a cough), the interviewers are to become distracted. They will suddenly forget all their good listening skills and conduct a sloppy interview. They should be aware of posture, voice tone, eye contact, etc.

13. Invite the absent members back to their groups.

14. Allow three minutes of good interviewing and three of poor.

15. Then ask the observers what they saw.

16. Ask the interviewed people how they felt, then explain the change in instructions.

17. Ask the persons doing the interviewing how it felt to switch to poor habits.

© Resource Publications, Inc.

Group Listening
Exercise (B)

1. Have participants break into pairs.

2. Have one person from each pair speak for five to ten minutes on a topic about which s/he has strong feelings. Ask the other person to listen carefully, using his/her best insights about effective listening.

3. Ask each participant to write an evaluation of the experience, using the following questions:

For the speaker:

What did the listener do that was helpful to me? What hindered me? In what ways did I experience being listened to? Did anything change in me as a result of being listened to? What?

For the listener:

Am I satisfied with my way of listening? Why or why not? Did I listen with love and a non- judgmental attitude? How did I show this attitude to the other?

4. Ask speaker and listener to share what they learned with each other and with the larger group. If there is time, repeat this exercise, with the participants taking the opposite roles.

Role Playing Exercise

1. Divide participants into small groups and ask each group to send one person from the room.

2. Ask each group to decide on a scenario into which a minister might be called (e.g., a family situation in which a teenager has just been killed in a car accident; a hospital room where a grandparent is dying; a home where a baby has just died from Sudden Infant Death Syndrome (crib death).

3. Have each group choose persons to be the characters in the scenario. Invite the person outside back into the room, and explain the scenario. This person is to make a pastoral visit, including a prayer or meaningful reference to faith, which will provide support for the hurting person.

4. If you have a large number of groups, ask one member of each to report back to the large group about their experience. Preferably, allow each group to do their role play in front of all the others. Then ask the players to tell the group how they felt in their characters' roles.

Lemon Exercise

The point of this exercise is to show that the bumps and wrinkles that will enable the participants to identify their own lemons make each lemon special. This is the same with people; our bumps and wrinkles make us special to God.

1. Place one lemon for each participant on a table and invite each person to take one. Give them five minutes to "get to know" their lemons. Ask them to look for distinguishing features, really concentrating on their lemons for the five minutes. They should not mark or deface their lemon in any way.

2. Place all the lemons in the bag and then roll them all out on the table again. Ask participants to claim their own lemons.

Scenarios for Discussion

1. A young husband commits suicide, leaving his wife with a small baby. How does the wife feel? How will the child feel when s/he grows up? (Stress that anger is normal and must be validated.)

2. The only child of a single mother is killed by a drunk driver. How will the mother feel? Perhaps the person needing your ministry will be the driver. How will you feel about that?

3. A family is gathered around the mother's deathbed. One daughter is hysterically upset, stating that she can't go on without Mother, they were so close. She displays obvious anger with her siblings, who do not seem so upset. What are possible reasons for this display? How might you help? How will you feel if you are not able to make things any better?

4. Parents receive the double shock of learning their son is gay and has AIDS. What might the parents feel? The son? What is each grieving for? How might you help?

Scenarios for Role Playing

1. It is the week before high school graduation. Tom, who will be graduating, has been terribly rude and belligerent around home all week. He also refuses to commit to any specific plans for after graduation. Mother decides she must speak with him.

2. Steve and Joan are divorced. Both of them are angry and terribly hurt, and they are pulling Michael, their ten-year-old son, in two. Each constantly hurls accusations at the other. You are the person who has been asked to help them find more constructive behaviors.

3. Elizabeth is twenty-nine years old. In the last ten years, she has risen to a position of responsibility and trust in a large corporation where she supervises over one hundred people. Now, after the birth of their second child, she and her husband have decided she should stay home for a few years. But Elizabeth develops claustrophobia. She cannot open the closet to take out clothing, cannot enter an elevator, cannot close the curtains and room doors at night. You are her friend and she has come to tell you how miserable she is. You know something about grief, and you also know that sometimes emotional pain can show up in unusual ways. You decide that you care enough about Elizabeth to try to help her find if there is a connection between her grief and her phobia. If so, you will refer her to a professional person for help. Remember, Elizabeth likely knows nothing about grief and does not even realize that she is grieving.

Grief Ministry Facilitator's Guide
© Resource Publications, Inc.

Appendix C:
Meditations

Pictures of Pain

This meditation is best read by two people. If you are team-teaching, this is a good chance to cooperate. If you are teaching alone, you might want to invite your guest speaker to assist you. Be sure to give the person a copy ahead of time to practice. *Do not ask one of your students to read; they need to experience the meditation.*

The speaking parts are marked Voice 1 and Voice 2. You are Voice 1 and your partner is Voice 2.

Turn down all lights and play soft instrumental background music. Ask participants to sit comfortably or lie on the floor, taking off glasses and loosening tight collars.

Eyes should be closed.

As you speak, be aware of your own voice; it must reach to all listeners but still be soft and low. This takes practice and you should read the entire meditation several times in privacy, testing your voice. If you are not sure, err on the side of being soft, and ask participants to silently raise a hand if you can't be heard.

Help participants to relax by asking them to become aware of the shape of their own bodies, where they come in contact with the environment (chairs, floor, flow of room air). Then continue:

> **Voice 1:** Now, feel the air as it swirls about your body, cool against your face, and into your nostrils. Follow it as it flows down into your lungs, swirling about to reach every surface, giving energizing oxygen to your blood. The blood, red and warm, flows through your body. Feel it flow to all areas of your body, relaxing tense muscles.

Pause.

> Which areas of your body are tired and tense? Let the warmth flowing through your body rest on those places, expanding and relaxing the muscles.

Pause.

Now, allow your mind to follow the pictures we will present to you. Move into each picture and, as much as you are able, become the characters. Feel what they feel.

Voice 2: I am a woman in Ethiopia [or Kuwait, or whatever part of the world is currently at war and starving]. Ten weeks ago I gave birth to twin daughters. Five days after the birthing, the soldiers came and said we must march toward the sunrise. So we left home, carrying our most precious things, our children. We also took a bag of cornmeal and some gourds filled with water. But we had no idea how far we must go. Within days, our food was gone. Soon, too, there was no more water. We tried to sleep in the day and walk at night, to avoid the sun. But often there were no trees or brush to shade us.

I have buried three children in these weeks, and now my breasts are dry, so I know my last baby will soon die too. We march from camp to camp, from hope to hope. Soon my husband and I will be two dried up old people, and we too shall return to the earth.

Voice 1: I live in Chicago. I just turned seventeen. My dad gave me a hunting rifle. "Every young man should have one," he said.

I walked by the frozen lake today, and I wondered how it would feel just to walk out into that icy whiteness and never come back. I know that not too far out, there's open water, wild and gray. That's the way I feel inside.

My parents don't care. I told my dad I was feeling really low, and he said, "Son, I have a board meeting tomorrow, and I have to get ready for it. You'll feel better soon." And my mom lives in Detroit with her new family. When I go there, I feel like a fifth wheel. Yesterday, my girlfriend told me she's making plans to go to California for college. I guess there's nobody who really needs me in their life.

Voice 2: I am a seventy-three-year-old woman. For over fifty years, I looked after my man. We raised our children and farmed our land side by side. It got harder the last few years, and then one night, I woke up and I couldn't talk or move my limbs any more. So they brought me to this place. I know my John is here, because each day he comes into the room and sits beside me, and tears roll down his cheeks. I want to reach out and hold him and tell him I understand; but it takes all my will just to squeeze his hand. I want to ask about the farm. Did they sell it, or is one of the children on

Grief Ministry Facilitator's Guide
© 1992 Resource Publications, Inc.

it? The children...Hah! Every week, the nurse carries in a new bouquet of flowers and puts it on the windowsill and reads off the names—one each week—I know the schedule. Andrew, then Mary, then Tim, and back to Andrew again. A few weeks ago, they all came and brought a poinsettia, so I knew Christmas was near. And they all sat around my bed and talked to each other—and about me! I wonder if they know I'm still here, inside this useless body. I wonder... I wonder.

Voice 1: My name is John and I'm seventy-five years old. I live in a nursing home. It's quite a change from running my own farm. But when my wife had a stroke, the kids insisted we come here to live. It's nice enough, I guess, if you like cards and craft games and silly old people. The walls are all pretty colors and there's lots of plants. I offered to look after the plants—I surely do know how—but they said they have a professional to do that. I thought I was a professional.

The kids have the farm now, Tim and his wife, Edith. I don't really mind that. I guess the hardest thing is seeing Martha. Every day, I go and sit beside her, and I hold her hand. I know she's in there. In that twisted old body is still the woman I married and loved—Oh! Did we love!—and lived with for a lifetime.

I want to tell her how I feel now, but I can't find the words. I want to ask how she feels, but I know she can't answer. So I usually don't say anything. After a while, I go and phone Mary and ask about the grandkids, and then I try to get involved in some activity—some stupid, empty activity.

Voice 2: I'm a young mother. It's funny, because I used to look forward to this stage of life, but now I don't seem to be experiencing any of the freedom and energy I expected. I wake up every day, and before I get out of bed, I know what my schedule will be: cooking and cleaning and changing diapers and reading to toddlers. Sometimes, I can keep them quiet with Sesame Street or Play-Doh. But most days, I feel as if there are constantly damp little people hanging on my legs. My husband is building a career and he leaves early and comes home late. I know he's working for us; but I wish he wouldn't complain when he finds toys around the house or the bathroom is messy. I miss my mother and my sisters so much, but there's no way we can move back east to be near them. I wish I had someone to talk to—someone tall enough to look me in the eyes!

© 1992 Resource Publications, Inc.

Voice 1: My name is Dorothy. I'm thirty-two years old and I just found out I have cancer. Not just any old cancer—one of those they call "terminal." The doctor was very kind, but as soon as he sat on my bed and held my hand, as soon as I heard his voice, I knew. He began by saying, "Dorothy, I'm sorry..." That was enough. I don't really remember what he said after that. Something about pain, and how they'd help me; he asked if I wanted to talk to a priest. How do I know who I want to talk to? All I know is I'll never see my kids graduate or get married. Tom and I won't have that trip to Russia we've been saving for. My parents—Strange! I never thought I'd die before them. Who will tell them? Who will tell the children? Will anyone understand what I'm experiencing, thinking, living? I feel so alone! Hello... Is anyone out there? *Help!*

Voice 2: Now, move back into your own body. Remember the points of stress you found at the beginning of this exercise. What color is the stress in your muscles? What is its shape? Picture your stress.

Pause.

What is your stress about? What parts of your life are painful? What are your wells of agony, your fonts of tears?

Pause.

Spend a few moments befriending your pain. Put an imaginary arm around yourself, especially the frightened, lonely part of you, the part you often ignore and push aside.

One minute of silence.

Now, without opening your eyes, look up. God is standing a few yards in front of you, smiling the kindest, most loving smile you've ever experienced. Now God is moving toward you, reaching out for you, kneeling beside you. God reaches and touches your cheek, stroking very, very softly.

Softly, God says, "Do you know that I have loved you since the beginning of time? Do you know that it was I who formed you in your parents' hearts and in your mother's womb, and it was I who cradled you as you left the womb and entered this life? Do you remember the times when you have been too hurt or exhausted to continue with life, and I have breathed into you with my breath? Have you received the messages of love which I have sent to you on the wind or in the rain or written on a frosted window pane?

You are my beloved. You I have dreamed and fashioned and called. You I have empowered through our love relationship, to bear witness in the world to that love.

I believe in you even when you do not believe in yourself. I am Love.

Pause.

Now God reaches out and touches your points of pain. God's touch is wonderfully gentle, like the waft of a feather, yet with it comes heat and vibration. The tension is leaving, is breaking down. It resists; the molecules of muscle tissue are fighting the soothing vibration. But as surely as the sun rises each morning, the tension must go. Only good can survive the touch of God.

Thirty seconds of silence.

Now, you are wonderfully cleansed and energized. You have never felt so whole and joyous and good. You feel perfectly integrated. When you are ready, open your eyes and return to the world.

After this meditation, leave the lights low and the music on. Allow a five-minute break in the session because people will be rather "spaced out" for a bit.

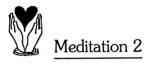
God Speaks

"I am God. I created you because I am love. I am passionately interested in you and I desire your growth. I only ask progress from you, not perfection. I am with you in your life and in your hunger to become more, to be more fully the person that I created you to be. You are unique; there is no one who has the same purpose in life that I have entrusted to you. I have a dream that you be only yourself, that you not try to be a carbon copy of someone else. You have your song to sing!

"Every flower blooms in its own time, in its unique fashion, in its own colors and scents; what matters to me is that it grows and blooms in its own unique way. So it is with you; the world will be missing something important and valuable if you do not live and become your truest self.

"What matters to me is that you are on your path of growth; that you are a bit further along tonight than you were this morning. I am with you if you fail; I know that you are trying. If you fall, I will reach out to you. I only ask that you relax in my love, take it easy, be happy with yourself, and believe in my love and hopes for you.

"You are the only you that will ever grace and gift this world, and the world is better for having you in it!"

Grief Ministry Facilitator's Guide
© 1992 Resource Publications, Inc.

Words to "Someone Who'll Stay"

The pain is all around me, it cuts me like a knife;
But I am a survivor and I'm fighting for my life.
I can read the fear within you, I see it in your eyes;
You're afraid that if you come too close,
My touch will turn to ice.

Don't run away, stay by my side;
Reach out your hand for the treasure inside.
It's okay to hurt, you're not in my way.
All that I need is someown who'll stay.

I can't make any promises or give much in return,
But if you'll share the seasons of my heart,
There's so much you can learn.
You will watch the spring unfolding at the freezing winter
snows
and you'll understand the reason
every thorn has its own rose.

Don't run away, stay by my side;
Reach out your hand for the treasure inside.
It's okay to hurt, you're not in my way.
All that I need is someown who'll stay.

Deanna Edwards. "Someone Who'll Stay." *Listen With Your Heart.* 777 East Walnut Stree, Provo, Utah 84604.

Grief Ministry Facilitator's Guide
© 1992 Resource Publications, Inc.

Appendix D:
Guest Speaker's Preparation Sheet

Guest Speaker's Preparation Sheet

1. Make a few notes about your personal background that you are willing to share.

2. What is the specific situation you are grieving at this time?

3. How long has it been since your loss?

4. What feelings did you have as soon as the loss happened?

5. Did you have any time to emotionally prepare for the loss? If so, what sort of feelings did you have during that time?

6. Have you had any physical symptoms of grief (upset stomach, intestinal upsets, headaches, fatigue, sleep problems, etc.)?

7. Has anyone been especially helpful? How have they helped? Be as specific as possible.

8. Has anyone blocked your moving through your grief, or made the journey more painful? How have they done this? Be as specific as possible.

9. Has God been important in your life? Has your perception of God changed because of your grief experience?

10. What would you tell people who want to help others who are experiencing what you have experienced?

© Resource Publications, Inc.

Appendix E:
Evaluation of Grief Ministry Training Program

Evaluation of Grief Ministry Training Program

1. When I began this program, I expected...

2. Did this program meet my needs for ministry preparation?

3. My favorite part of the program was...

4. I grew most when we...

5. I was challenged most by...

6. Please rate these factors on a scale of one to ten, one being unacceptable and ten being great:

Facilitation (Leadership)	1 2 3 4 5 6 7 8 9 10
Environment (room, lighting, etc.)	1 2 3 4 5 6 7 8 9 10
Scripture Sharing	1 2 3 4 5 6 7 8 9 10
Meditation and Prayer	1 2 3 4 5 6 7 8 9 10
Academic Content	1 2 3 4 5 6 7 8 9 10
Handouts	1 2 3 4 5 6 7 8 9 10
Group Participation	1 2 3 4 5 6 7 8 9 10

7. Do you have any suggestions for change if we present this program again?

Appendix F:
Prayer Request Card

Prayer Request Card

Fill out the prayer card below and send to:

Donna Reilly Williams, Pastoral Consultant
18327 147th Court N.E.
Woodinville, WA 98072

> **We will be presenting a program to train _____ ministers to the grieving at:**
>
> **Institution:** _____
>
> **Address:** _____
>
> **Facilitator:** _____
>
> **Dates: From_____ to _____**
>
> *Please pray for us!*

Audio Cassettes

Edwards, Deanna. *Listen With Your Heart.* 777 E. Walnut Street, Provo, Utah 84604.

_____. *Peacebird.* Same information as above.

Talbot, John Michael. *Quiet Reflections.* Sparrow Records, 9255 Deering Avenue, Chatsworth, California 91311.

Filmstrips

Continuing the Ministry of Jesus. Alba House Communications, 7050 Pinehurst, Dearborn, Michigan 48126.

If I Should Die Before I Wake. Presbyterian Health, Education, and Welfare Association, 100 Witherspoon Street, Room 3041, Louisville, Kentucky 40203-1396.

Prayer Is Listening. From the series of filmstrips entitled *Prayer.* Brown-ROA, P.O. Box 539, Dubuque, Iowa 52004-0539.

Video Cassettes

Reeves, Nancy, Ph.D. *When A Baby Dies.* Island Loss Clinic, 2910 Dean Avenue, Victoria, British Columbia, Canada V8R 4Y4.

Teach Me To Die. Franciscan Communications, 1229 South Santee Street, Los Angeles, California 90015.

Use This Ad to Replenish Your
Grief Ministry Textbook Supply

Copy the coupon below every time you need to re-order textbooks for your Grief Ministry facilitator's program.

Plus, if you're planning to stock up now for future programs, take advantage of our special quantity discount offer:

- **10 - 24 books = 10% discount**
- **25 - 49 books = 20% discount**
- **50 + books = 30% discount**

In addition, we're pleased to announce the release of the **revised and expanded** edition of *Grief Ministry: Helping Others Mourn*. This already-indispensable guide now includes chapters on AIDS and job loss.

Don't let your supply run out—order now!

Grief Ministry: Helping Others Mourn
Revised and Expanded

Donna Reilly Williams & JoAnn Sturzl

Paperbound, $14.95
215 pages, 5½" x 8½"
ISBN 0-89390-233-0

- -

Order Form 1-888-273-7782

Copy and fill out the order form below, and return to Resource Publications, Inc., 160 East Virginia Street #290, San Jose, California 95112-5876. Call (800) 736-7600 or FAX (408) 287-8748.

☐ Yes! I want to take advantage of your quantity discount.

Quantity   Price   Total

_____ *Grief Ministry: Helping Others Mourn*   _____ _____
            Revised and Expanded

Name _____   Quantity Discount _____
Institution _____   Sales tax* _____
Address_____   Shipping** _____
City/State/ZIP _____   Total amount enclosed _____

☐ My check or purchase order is enclosed.
☐ Charge my ☐ VISA ☐ MC

Card #_____-_____-_____-_____   * California residents add 7¼% sales tax (Santa Clara
                                              County residents add 8¼%.

Expiration date_____   ** $2 for orders up to $20. 10% of order for orders over
                                              $20 but less than $150. $15 for orders of $150 or more.

Signature_____   GF

Improve Your Group Facilitation Skills!

Leadership Skills for Peer Group Facilitators

Joan Sturkie & Charles Hanson, Ph.D.

Paperbound, $11.95, 144 pages, 5½" x 8 ½"
ISBN 0-89390-232-2
April 1992

This handy guidebook will help you master the skills you need for successful group leadership. Includes insights on the following:

- **Setting up a program**
- **Keeping the group going**
- **Communicating effectively**
- **Encouraging interaction between group members**
- **Empowering the group to accomplish its goals**

The author discusses the pitfalls of leading a group—and shares her solutions to dealing with common problems. Beginners will find this an invaluable companion as they pioneer their new group leadership responsibilities. Veteran leaders will find new insights for making their programs even better!

The Pressure's Off!

Partners in Healing: Redistributing the Power in Counselor-Client Relationships

Barbara Friedman, Ph.D.

Paperbound, $14.95, 193 pages, 5½" x 8½"
ISBN 0-89390-226-8
April 1992

You don't have to be a "power figure" in your group or when you're one-on-one with your participants. Rather, the author says, it's a give and take. You empower them; they empower you.

It sounds revolutionary because it is, literally. The pattern throughout history shows people going full circle in their collective relationship—from being one with each other, to insisting on being separate and unconnected, back to the realization that people are connected and equal by design.

And the counselor-client relationship is no different. You the counselor don't have to have all the answers. And your clients don't have to wait for your advice. It's a *mutual* discovery process that can be rewarding for everyone involved—just read the Anecdotes chapter!

Order from your local bookseller, or use the order form on the last page.

More Ministry Resources...

MOMS: Developing a Program

Paula Hagen & Patricia Hoyt

Paperbound, $19.95
132 pages, 7" x 10"
ISBN 0-89390-228-4
April 1992

MOMS: A Personal Journal

Paula Hagen with Vickie LoPiccolo Jennett

Paperbound, $9.95
112 pages, 7" x 10"
ISBN 0-89390-224-1

This program along with its companion *Journal* compose a six-week experience for mothers or any women who need inspiration, encouragement, and affirmation. Designed as a spirituality program to develop self-esteem, self-awareness, and self-sacredness, the Ministry of Mothers Sharing is an opportunity for women to reflect on their experiences, share their stories, and realize more fully their personal family ministry. The guide includes sample budget and organizational chart for starting your program; lesson plans; prayer rituals; and all the supplementary materials you'll need.

Ministry in a Messy World

Jerry Welte

Paperbound, $9.95
274 pages, 5½" x 8½"
ISBN 0-89390-154-7

Get in touch with the desperation and hopelessness that characterize many human lives—lives you come in contact with every day. This book defines the mess you're up against, then offers you realistic suggestions (and lots of hope) for your ministry.

Order from your local bookseller, or use the order form on the last page.

More Ministry Resources... (continued)

Gem of the First Water:
A Recovery Process
for Troubled Teenagers

Ron Phillips

Paperbound, $14.95
229 pages, 5½" x 8½"
ISBN 0-89390-181-4

Part of growing up is accepting responsibility for our actions. Help the teenagers in your ministry get through this troubling time in their lives. Let them read this book and you'll see instant results: they'll consider the consequences of their actions and start making consistently good decisions.

Teenage Mothers:
Their Experience,
Strength, and Hope

Andre Beauchamp

Paperbound, $8.95
80 pages, 5½" x 8½"
Photographs
ISBN 0-89390-180-6

Need to give a teenage mother or mother-to-be smoe hope and support? Here is the perfect book! With it, she can take courage form those who have been there and have grown from the experience. Based on interviews with the many single mothers served by the Miserecordia Sisters, Andre Beauchamp gives an honest picture of what teenage mothers experience today: their struggles, their hopes, their sorrows, their discoveries, and their joys. Very nice tender approach.

- -

Order Form

Order from your local bookseller, or mail this form to Resource Publications, Inc., 160 E. Virginia St., #290, San Jose, CA 95112-5876, (408) 286-8505, FAX (408) 287-8748.

Qty.	Title	Price	Total
---	-----------------------	-------	-------
---	-----------------------	-------	-------
---	-----------------------	-------	-------
---	-----------------------	-------	-------

☐ My check/purchase order is enclosed.
☐ Charge my ☐ VISA ☐ MC.

Expiration Date _____
Card # _____-_____-_____-_____

Subtotal _____
California residents add 7¼% sales tax
(8¼% in Santa Clara County) _____
Postage & handling* _____
Total amount enclosed _____

Signature_____
Name _____
Institution _____
Street _____
C/S/Z_____

*Postage & handling: $2 for orders up to $20; 10% of order for orders over $20 but less than $150; $15 for orders of $150 or more.

GG